Efficient Mutual Fund Markets

This book covers a new and innovative approach to the issue of investment portfolio efficiency from the perspective of a large institutional investor. It discusses the challenges relating to changes in returns on the international stock market, with particular emphasis on investments.

Instead of focusing on just one designated market, the book examines four diversified, developed markets, and models the Polish market as a representative of emerging markets. The authors argue that the current market for available financial instruments, mainly derivatives, may be an example of a partially complete market. With such assumptions, they test selected markets, assuming that a representative investor, such as an investment fund, makes rational decisions and uses all available financial instruments. The research conducted in the book is unique in its assumption that investors form portfolios that consider the structure of the company's financial results. The significant impact that the financial crisis in the United States since 2007, the COVID-19 pandemic, and Russia's aggression against Ukraine have had on investors' decisions is also discussed.

The book will find an audience among researchers, scholars, and students specialising in finance and capital market investments.

Stanisław Urbański is a Professor in the Department of Finance and Accounting and Head of the Capital Markets Laboratory, AGH University of Krakow, Cracow, Poland.

Bartosz Rymkiewicz is an Assistant Professor in the Department of Finance and Accounting, AGH University of Krakow, Cracow, Poland.

Jacek Leśkow is the Rector of American University in Kyiv, Ukraine, and Professor of Cracow University of Technology, Cracow, Poland.

Bartosz Stawiarski is an Assistant Professor in the Department of Applied Mathematics, Faculty of Computer Science and Telecommunications, Cracow University of Technology, Cracow, Poland.

Routledge Focus on Economics and Finance

The fields of economics are constantly expanding and evolving. This growth presents challenges for readers trying to keep up with the latest important insights. Routledge Focus on Economics and Finance presents short books on the latest big topics, linking in with the most cutting-edge economics research.

Individually, each title in the series provides coverage of a key academic topic, whilst collectively the series forms a comprehensive collection across the whole spectrum of economics.

Health insurance in the United States of America
Austrian Perspectives on Interventionism before ObamaCare
Łukasz Jasiński

Financing for Development
Towards a New, Green Bretton Woods
Stefan Brunnhuber

Efficient Mutual Fund Markets
A Global Perspective
Stanisław Urbański, Bartosz Rymkiewicz, Jacek Leśkow and Bartosz Stawiarski

For more information about this series, please visit: www.routledge.com/Routledge-Focus-on-Economics-and-Finance/book-series/RFEF

Efficient Mutual Fund Markets

A Global Perspective

Stanisław Urbański,
Bartosz Rymkiewicz, Jacek Leśkow
and Bartosz Stawiarski

Routledge
Taylor & Francis Group
LONDON AND NEW YORK

First published 2026
by Routledge
4 Park Square, Milton Park, Abingdon, Oxon OX14 4RN

and by Routledge
605 Third Avenue, New York, NY 10158

Routledge is an imprint of the Taylor & Francis Group, an informa business

British Library Cataloguing-in-Publication Data
A catalogue record for this book is available from the British Library

ISBN: 978-1-032-95959-7 (hbk)
ISBN: 978-1-032-95960-3 (pbk)
ISBN: 978-1-003-58733-0 (ebk)

DOI: 10.4324/9781003587330

Typeset in Times New Roman
by Newgen Publishing UK

Contents

Figures

Tables

Acknowledgements

The authors of this book would like to thank

Dimitris N. Politis
Distinguished Professor of Mathematics and Data Science
Halicioglu Data Science Institute Chancellor's Endowed Chair II
University of California, San Diego
La Jolla, CA 92093-0112, USA

and

Piotr S. Kokoszka
Professor of Statistics
Fellow of the Institute of Mathematical Statistics
Department of Statistics
Colorado State University
Fort Collins, CO 80523-1877, USA

for their detailed reviews.

Stanisław Urbański would like to thank his sons Kacper and Karol for their encouragement and support in conducting the research presented in this book.

Bartosz Rymkiewicz would like to express his sincere gratitude to Dear Iwona for her support while working on this book.

Jacek Leśkow would like to express his deepest thanks to his wife, Dorothy, for her constant support and love while this book was prepared. Research project partially supported by the program "Excellence initiative – research university" for the AGH University of Krakow.

1 Introduction

This book introduces an innovative approach to investment portfolio efficiency, focusing on large institutional investors. It addresses issues related to changes in returns on international stock markets, particularly investments made by large institutional investors, such as investment funds. Theoretically, grounded investment guidelines for such investors are based on the work of Fama and French (1993) (hereafter FF1993), which introduced the renowned 3-factor and 5-factor stock and bond pricing models. In these models, the authors define state variables and propose HML and SMB risk factors, which can model future economic states and returns. Two years later, Fama and French (1995) (hereafter FF1995) extended this work by identifying additional state variables that indirectly generate HML, SMB, and, ultimately, returns. FF1995 found that the key state variable influencing future economic states is the structure of a company's past financial results relative to its equity capital. These risk factors, defined by the state variable, allow for forecasting future asset prices.

However, the FF1995 framework has not been updated by Fama and French using new state variables. Their 2015 model introduces only two new factors, which are not derived from their 1995 study. To the authors' knowledge, no other applications of the ICAPM, including the Fama and French model augmented with the momentum factor (Carhart 1997), incorporate the state variables presented in FF1995.

Incorporating the pricing model from FF1995 addresses the research gap concerning the estimation of future asset returns. This study examines the changes in the return/risk relationship of stocks traded in American, European, Japanese, Chinese, and emerging markets, with a particular focus on the Polish market. The research

DOI: 10.4324/9781003587330-1

challenges the widely accepted paradigm of Jensen (1978), as revisited by Malkiel (2016), which suggests that ex-post fundamental analysis does not lead to above-average investment returns. We define above-average returns as those earned by fundamentally designed portfolios relative to benchmark market portfolios. Our research focuses on conditional market efficiency tests, from the perspective of a representative investor. This investor forecasts risk factors that model the state variables influencing future returns. We assume the representative investor is a large institutional investor.

Related literature. The efficient market hypothesis (EMH) has been discussed in the literature since the late 1950s by Roberts (1959), Fama (1965a,1965b), and Samuelson (1965a). The concept of EMH arose from an attempt to explain the random nature of prices as a result of a rational market.

To demonstrate this randomness, various probabilistic models are employed, such as the Random Walk Model (Fama 1965a) and the Martingale Model (Samuelson 1965b). Samuelson and Mandelbrot emphasised that random price fluctuations occur in a market where all participants have equal access to information (Boldt and Arbit 1984; Mandelbrot 1966). Fama (1965b) defines an efficient market as 'a market where there are large numbers of rational profit-maximisers actively competing, each trying to predict future market values of individual securities, and where important current information is almost freely available to all participants'. An efficient market is one in which prices fully reflect available information (Fama 1970). An example of such a market assumes three conditions: no transaction costs, free access to all available information for market participants, and a clear relationship between available information, current prices, and future price distributions (Fama 1970). Malkiel (2003) further defines efficient financial markets as those in which 'investors cannot earn above-average returns without accepting above-average risks'. However, it is suggested that perfect market efficiency is unattainable, as it would eliminate the incentive for professional entities to gather information reflected in market prices (Malkiel 2003). The existence of an efficient market where obtaining information incurs costs would undermine competitive markets, as rational investors would have no incentive to pay for information (Grossman and Stiglitz 1980).

Jensen (1978) argues that the EMH is an extension of the zero-profit competitive equilibrium condition from classical price theory, applied to the dynamic behaviour of prices in speculative markets under uncertainty. It posits that a market is efficient with respect to a specific set of information if no economic benefits can be obtained by exploiting that information.

Fama (1970) categorises market efficiency into three forms: strong, semi-strong, and weak. In the weak form of market efficiency, the only available information is historical prices. Hence, strategies based on technical analysis cannot yield above-average profits (Malkiel 1989). This form aligns with the 'Random Walk Hypothesis' (Malkiel 1989), which asserts that 'an efficient market is one where large numbers of rational, profit-maximisers actively compete, with each trying to predict future market values of individual securities, and where important current information is almost freely available to all participants'. Thus, in an efficient market, 'the actual price of a security at any point in time will be a good estimate of its intrinsic value' (Fama 1965b). It is 'a price series where all subsequent price changes represent random departures from previous prices' (Malkiel 2003). Verification of the weak form of the hypothesis is based on tests of return predictability, including cross-sectional predictability and seasonal return patterns (Fama 1991). The validity of the weak-form EMH has been demonstrated in several studies, including Goel and Sahay (2023), who examined the Indian Carbonex and Greenex indices from June 3, 2013, to December 31, 2020, using Augmented Dickey-Fuller, normality, and autocorrelation tests. Stanley et al. (2021) also supported the weak-form EMH for DJIA component stocks from 1978 to 2018 through two strategies. Using parametric and non-parametric variance ratio tests, Hung et al. (2009) found support for the weak-form EMH in large-cap stocks of the TOPIX and FTSE indices. In contrast, Rosenberg and Rudd (1982) showed that market inefficiency exists in the weak form, demonstrating a statistically significant correlation between components of monthly security returns using a multifactor return model. Gurung and Sarkar (2023) found that the random walk hypothesis and EMH did not hold for the BSE Green Index of the Indian stock market. Ogiemudia and Isibor (2021), using OLS regression, serial correlation tests, the runs test (RT), and the Kolmogorov–Smirnov (K-S) test, demonstrated inefficiency in the Nigerian Bourse from 1985 to 2019. Ali et al. (2021) showed inefficiency in Pakistan's KSE-100 and KSE-30 indices from January 1, 2014, to August 28, 2019, using serial correlation tests, the RT, and Box-Ljung Statistics. Hung et al. (2009) also rejected the weak-form EMH for small-cap stocks in the TOPIX and FTSE indices.

The semi-strong form of market efficiency assumes that prices adjust rapidly to all publicly available information, such as announcements of annual profits. The marginal benefits of acting on such information do not exceed the marginal costs, meaning that fundamental analysis cannot yield above-average profits (Malkiel 2016). This form is widely accepted as the standard paradigm (Jensen 1978). Tests to verify this hypothesis, known as event studies, examine how prices react to unexpected news. If prices do not respond, it indicates that the news is already incorporated into the price, rendering it uninformative for the market (McKenzie 2008). Typical events studied include stock splits, dividend changes, or earnings reports (Boldt and Arbit 1984). Another approach uses forecasting models: in an efficient market, there should be no systematic relationship between current forecast errors and past errors in the information set. If a forecasting model outperforms the futures price as a predictor of cash prices, the EMH must be rejected (Goss et al. 1992).

The correctness of the semi-strong form of the EMH has been demonstrated by various studies, including McKenzie (2008), who showed that futures prices continue to react to USDA report releases. Fama et al. (1969) found that, on average, the market fully reflects information about stock splits, with price adjustments occurring only to the extent that they signal changes in expected future dividends. Reilly and Drzycimski (1981), analysing 130 NYSE-listed companies whose shares underwent a two-for-one split between 1964 and 1976, concluded that stock prices adjust before or shortly after the public announcement and that above-average returns are unavailable to the general public or professionals due to transaction costs. Groenewold (1997) tested market efficiency in the Statex Actuaries' Price Index for Australia and the NZSE-40 Index for New Zealand using cointegration and Granger causality tests. Chu and Lim (1998) demonstrated, through a regression study based on Anderson and Peterson's modified efficiency results, that stock prices in Singapore reflect profit efficiency more than cost efficiency, suggesting market efficiency. Khan and Ikram (2010) found that the Indian capital market, represented by the National Stock Exchange and Bombay Stock Exchange, is semi-strong efficient, as foreign investments significantly impact market behaviour. Bulski and Górski (2012) found no grounds to reject the semi-strong efficiency of the Polish market (WSE) in the long term, as above-average profits could not be achieved. However, Basu (1977) argued against this form of efficiency, showing that NYSE prices do not fully reflect P/E ratio information, indicating market inefficiency. He noted that, despite high transaction costs, the difficulty in earning above-average profits does not conclusively disprove the semi-strong efficiency hypothesis. Leuthold and Hartmann (1979, 1980) identified inefficiency in the Hog Future Market, while Rose and Selody (1984) found inefficiency in the Canada-USA market using a test for inter-forward market trade. Agrawal (2007), studying the impact of monetary policy announcements, also showed the inefficiency of the Indian CNX Nifty index. Kubacki (2017), using event studies, found that the Polish, Czech, and UK markets are inefficient. Conversely, Goss et al. (1992), using a forecasting model, found no evidence to reject the semi-strong market efficiency hypothesis for the US Oats Market.

The strong form of EMH, by contrast, focuses on price-relevant information that is accessible only to certain investors, such as insiders or specialists (Fama 1970). This form is generally viewed as theoretical and extreme (Jensen 1978). Fuller and Farrell (1987) distinguish between the super-strong and near-strong forms of EMH. The super-strong form asserts that security prices incorporate all information available exclusively to insiders and exchange specialists. The near-strong form posits that prices reflect all private estimates based on public information (Mallikarjunappa and Manjunatha 2009). Fama (1991) refers to tests of private information as those verifying the strong form of EMH. Commonly used tests include comparing the performance of mutual funds with a benchmark portfolio, such as a stock market index (Gupta et al. 2008). Gupta et al. (2008) demonstrated the strong form of EMH, showing that fund managers with better information, including insider information, do not outperform randomly selected portfolios. In contrast, Jaffe (1974) challenged this view, noting that insider trading prior to share splits can yield significant returns over an 8-month period, although high transaction costs (around 40% of gross profits) undermine market efficiency. Reilly and Drzycimski (1981) also found that investors with insider information about forthcoming split announcements achieve above-average returns for NYSE-listed companies undergoing two-for-one splits.

In Chapter 2, we explore several key applications of ICAPM theory published at the turn of the 20th and 21st centuries. We critically assess specific asset pricing applications, focusing on the modified Fama and French model proposed by Urbański (2012) and later by Urbański and

Zarzecki (2022). Additionally, we examine the relationship between market efficiency and pricing accuracy in light of the ICAPM.[1]

In Chapter 3, we present practical pricing procedures under the ICAPM framework. In Section 3.1, we introduce the fundamental model for constructing investment portfolios, following the results of FF1995. Section 3.2 outlines selected applications of equilibrium price modelling within the ICAPM context, along with necessary tests to ensure that the modelled returns are consistent with ICAPM predictions. This section also includes a comparison of pricing consistency across three selected applications. Section 3.3 discusses selected pricing applications supplemented with sustainability-sensitive factors. In Sections 3.4 and 3.5, we detail procedures for estimating the parameters of the pricing applications and methods used to assess the efficiency hypotheses proposed for the examined markets. Based on this analysis, we design innovative tests to verify the hypothesis that the average return and risk of the portfolios generated are competitive with benchmark portfolios.

Chapter 4 presents the data used for calculations and outlines the scope of the research. Chapter 5 reports the results of the calculations and statistical analysis of the observed changes across the studied markets. Chapter 6 provides financial interpretations of the obtained results, while Chapter 7 offers a summary and conclusions. The final chapter discusses the research limitations and proposes directions for future studies.

Note

1 According to Merton's ICAPM, future asset prices are determined by the future states of the economy. An accurate forecast of the risk factors that model these future states enables the estimation of future returns.

References

Agrawal, G. (2007). Monetary Policy Announcements and Stock Price Behavior: Empirical Evidence from CNX Nifty. *Decision* 34 (2), 133–153.

Ali, S.B., Farooq, K. Shah, Z.A., & Burney, S. (2021). Testing the Evidence on Weak Form EMH at Pakistan Stock Market. *Turkish Online Journal of Qualitative Inquiry (TOJQI)* 12 (8), 5147–5153.

Basu, S. (1977). Investment Performance of Common Stocks in Relation to Their Price-Earnings Ratios: A Test of the Efficient Market Hypothesis. *Journal of Finance* 32 (3), 663–682.

Boldt, B.L., & Arbit, H.L. (1984). Efficient Markets and Professional Investor. *Financial Analysts Journal* 40 (4), 22–34.

Bulski, D., & Górski, M. (2012). Wyniki testów hipotezy półsilnej efektywności informacyjnej Giełdy Papierów Wartościowych w Warszawie w latach 2005–2011. *Problemy Zarządzania* 10/4 (1), 141–168.

Carhart, M.M. (1997). On Persistence in Mutual Fund Performance. *Journal of Finance* 52 (1), 57–82.

Chu, S.F., & Lim G.H. (1998). Share Performance and Profit Efficiency of Banks in an Oligopolistic Market: Evidence from Singapore. *Journal of Multinational Financial Management* 8, 155–168.

Fama, E.F. (1965a). The Behavior of Stock-Market Prices. *Journal of Business* 38 (1), 34–105.

Fama, E.F. (1965b). Random Walks in Stock-Market Prices. *Financial Analysts Journal* 21 (5), 55–59.

Fama, E.F. (1970). Efficient Capital Markets: a Review of Theory and Empirical Work. *Journal of Finance* 25 (2), 383–417.

Fama, E.F. (1991). Efficient Capital Market: II. *Journal of Finance* 46 (5), 1575–1617.

Fama, E.F., Fisher, L., Jensen, M.C., & Roll, R. (1969). The Adjustment of Stock Prices to New Information. *International Economic Review* 10 (1), 1–21.

Fama, E.F., & French, K.R. (1993). Common Risk Factors in the Returns on Stocks and Bonds. *Journal of Financial Economics* 33, 3–56.

Fama, E.F., & French, K.R. (1995). Size and Book-to-Market Factors in Earnings and Returns. *Journal of Finance* 50 (1), 131–155.

Fuller, R.J., & Farrell, J.L. (1987). *Modern Investments and Security Analysis*. New York: McGraw-Hill.

Goel, A., & Sahay, N. (2023). Investigating the Market Efficiency of Socially Responsible Indices: Evidence from India. *International Journal of Finance, Economics and Business* 2 (4), 301–312.

Goss, B.A., Avsar, S.G., & Chan, S.C. (1992). Rational Expectations and Price Determination in the US Oats Market. *Economic Record* 68, 16–26.

Groenewold, N. (1997). Share Market Efficiency: Tests Using Daily Data for Australia and New Zealand. *Applied Financial Economics* 7 (6), 645–657.

Grossman, S.J., & Stiglitz, J.E. (1980). On the Impossibility of Informationally Efficient Markets. *American Economic Review* 70 (3), 393–408.

Gupta, D., Anand, A., & Singh, R. (2008). Empirical Testing of Strong Form of Market Efficiency. *Asia-Pacific Business Review* 4 (3), 53–59.

Gurung, P., & Sarkar, S. (2023). Testing of Market Efficiency of BSE GREENEX: An Empirical Analysis. *SDMIMD Journal of Management* 14 (1), 91–106.

Hung, J.-C., Lee, Y.-H., & Pai, T.-Y. (2009). Examining Market Efficiency for Large- and Small-Capitalization of TOPIX and FTSE Stock Indices. *Applied Financial Economics* 19, 735–744.

Jaffe, J.F. (1974). Special Information and Insider Trading. *Journal of Business* 47 (3), 410–428.

Jensen, M.C. (1978). Some Anomalous Evidence Regarding Market Efficiency. *Journal of Financial Economics* 6 (2/3), 95–101.

Khan, A. Q., & Ikram, S. (2010). Testing Semi-Strong Form of Efficient Market Hypothesis in Relation to the Impact of Foreign Institutional Investors' (FII's) Investments on Indian Capital Market. *International Journal of Trade, Economics and Finance* 1 (4), 373–379.

Kubacki, D. (2017). Porównanie efektywności informacyjnej rynku finansowego w wybranych krajach Unii Europejskiej. *Finanse, Rynki Finansowe, Ubezpieczenia* 2 (86), 123–133.

Leuthold, R.M., & Hartmann, P.A. (1979). A Semi-Strong Form Evaluation of the Efficiency of the Hog Futures Market. *American Journal of Agricultural Economics* 61 (3), 482–489.

Leuthold, R.M., & Hartmann, P.A. (1980). A Semi-Strong Form Evaluation of the Efficiency of the Hog Futures Market: Reply. *American Journal of Agricultural Economics* 62 (3), 585–587.

Malkiel, B.G. (1989). Efficient Market Hypothesis. In J. Eatwell et al. (eds), *Finance. The New Palgrave*. London: Palgrave Macmillan, 127–134.

Malkiel, B.G. (2003). The Efficient Market Hypothesis and Its Critics. *Journal of Economic Perspective* 17 (1), 59–82.

Malkiel, B.G. (2016). *A Random Walk Down Wall Street, The Time-Tested Strategy for Successful Investing*, New York: W.W. Norton.

Mallikarjunappa, T., & Manjunatha, T. (2009). Stock Price Reactions to Dividend Announcements. *Journal of Management & Public Policy* 1 (1), 43–56.

Mandelbrot, B. (1966). Forecasts of Future Prices, Unbiased Markets, and Martingale Models. *Journal of Business* 39 (1), 242–255.

McKenzie, A.M. (2008). Pre-Harvest Price Expectations for Corn: The Information Content of USDA Reports and New Crop Futures. *American Journal of Agricultural Economics* 90 (2), 351–366.

Ogiemudia, O., & Isibor, E. (2021). Testing Weak Form of Efficient Market Hypothesis (EMH) in Nigeria. *Journal of Academic Research In Economics* 13 (3), 488–508.

Reilly, F.K., & Drzycimski, E.F. (1981). Short-Run Profits from Stock Splits. *Financial Management* 10 (3), 64–74.

Roberts, H.V. (1959). Stock-Market Patterns and Financial Analysis: Methodological Suggestions. *Journal of Finance* 14 (1), 1–10.

Rose, A.K., & Selody, J.G. (1984). Exchange Market Efficiency: A Semi-Strong Test Using Multiple Markets and Daily Data. *Review of Economics and Statistics* 66 (4), 669–672.

Rosenberg, B., & Rudd, A. (1982). Factor Related and Specific Returns of Common Stocks: Serial Correlation and Market Efficiency. *Journal of Finance* 37, 543–554.

Samuelson, P.A. (1965a). Rational Theory of Warrant Pricing. *Industrial Management Review* 6 (2), 13–39.

Samuelson, P.A. (1965b). Proof that Properly Anticipated Prices Fluctuate Randomly. *Industrial Management Review* 6 (2), 41–49.

Stanley, D.J., Kinsman, M.D., Kownatzki, C., & DiLellio, J. (2021). Is the Dow Jones Industrial Average Even Weak-Form Market Efficient? *Journal of Accounting & Finance* 21 (1), 159–171.

Urbański, S. (2012). Multifactor Explanations of Returns on the Warsaw Stock Exchange in Light of the ICAPM. *Economic Systems* 36 (4), 552–570.

Urbański, S., & Zarzecki, D. (2022). The Fama-French Model for Estimating the Cost of Equity Capital: The Impact of Real Options of Investment Projects. *Economic Systems* 46 (1), 100874.

2 Theoretical ICAPM considerations

The classical Capital Asset Pricing Model (CAPM), proposed by Treynor (1962), Sharpe (1964), Lintner (1965), and Mossin (1966), along with Merton's Intertemporal CAPM (ICAPM) (1973), defines a set of efficient portfolios. These portfolios, situated on the Capital Market Line (CML) in the risk-return space, generate the maximum possible return for a given level of risk. As such, a rational investor forms portfolios located along the CML. The asset pricing model proposed by FF1993 is an example of the ICAPM. Merton (1973) asserts that his model accurately prices future returns in a complete market – one where financial instruments exist to hedge all investor positions. Merton further posits that future returns are determined by the states of the economy, which, in a complete market, can be secured by selected financial instruments. The factors reflecting the roles of these instruments, while simultaneously modelling future economic states, serve as the explanatory variables of the ICAPM.[1]

FF1993 identifies the HML and SMB factors as proxies for future economic states. However, in their subsequent work (FF1995), they argue that the factors generating future returns are not HML and SMB, but rather the company's past financial performance relative to equity capital.

The research presented here differs by assuming that investors form portfolios based on the structure of a company's past financial results relative to equity. Two modifications of the FF1993 model are presented by the first author of this work: Urbański (2012, MFF2012) and Urbański and Zarzecki (2022, MFF2022). These

DOI: 10.4324/9781003587330-2

proposals represent innovative applications of the ICAPM, grounded in the fundamental functional (FUN) described in Section 3.1 of Chapter 3, which models future economic states. The applications, which integrate the recommendations of FF1995, are briefly outlined in Chapter 3. They aim to fill the gap in the substantive understanding of stock market returns.

The explanatory variables of the model are derived from the values of FUN, which reflects the structure of past financial results. This function incorporates both evaluation and pricing factors for companies listed on the market. A hypothetical investor can predict future returns accurately, provided they can forecast the economic states that will determine the future value of assets. If investment simulations based on FUN successfully predict future returns, it suggests a relationship between FUN and both known and novel investment strategies that consider future economic conditions. In other words, the FUN functional defines state variables that enable the securing of future investment returns. Thus, it can be argued that the risk factors based on FUN predict future states and generate future returns. The proposed pricing application, grounded in these factors, meets the primary criterion of Merton's ICAPM theory, with returns from the generated portfolios expected to lie on the CML.

Building on this reasoning, we conclude that the market in which an investor forms portfolios based on FUN represents an efficient market, in line with the ICAPM framework.

A pertinent question arises: what form of market efficiency, according to Fama's theory (Fama 1970), is generated by risk factors based on FUN? If the ICAPM investor constructs portfolios using FUN, which is based on financial results prior to the official announcement of the most recent reporting period, the market for the resulting returns should exhibit strong-form efficiency. In practice, such a FUN functional could be based on forecasts of financial results derived from published consensus. However, if the ICAPM investor forms portfolios using FUN, which is based on financial results published after the official announcement, the market for the resulting returns should exhibit semi-strong form efficiency. If the portfolios formed on FUN do not display the characteristics of an efficient market, it can be concluded that the investor is not adhering to the ICAPM framework.

Note

1 The modern financial instruments market is a partially complete market. For instance, derivatives can be used to hedge against changes in exchange rates, interest rates, or to protect the value of an asset portfolio.

References

Fama, E.F. (1970). Efficient Capital Markets: a Review of Theory and Empirical Work. *Journal of Finance* 25 (2), 383–417.

Fama, E.F., & French, K.R. (1993). Common Risk Factors in the Returns on Stocks and Bonds. *Journal of Financial Economics* 33, 3–56.

Fama, E.F., & French, K.R. (1995). Size and Book-to-Market Factors in Earnings and Returns. *Journal of Finance* 50 (1), 131–155.

Lintner J. (1965). The Valuation of Risk Assets and the Selection of Risky Investments in Stock Portfolios and Capital Budgets. *Review of Economics and Statistics* 47 (1), 13–37.

Merton, R.C. (1973). An Intertemporal Capital Asset Pricing Model. *Econometrica* 41 (5), 867–888.

Mossin, J. (1966). Equilibrium in a Capital Asset Market. *Econometrica* 34 (4), 768–783.

Sharpe, W.F. (1964). Capital Asset Prices: A Theory of Market Equilibrium under Conditions of Risk. *Journal of Finance* 19 (3), 425–442.

Treynor, J.L. (1962). Toward a Theory of Market Value of Risky Assets. Unpublished Manuscript, 6. Available at SSRN: https://ssrn.com/abstract=628187 or http://dx.doi.org/10.2139/ssrn.628187

Urbański, S. (2012). Multifactor Explanations of Returns on the Warsaw Stock Exchange in Light of the ICAPM. *Economic Systems* 36 (4), 552–570.

Urbański, S., & Zarzecki, D. (2022). The Fama-French Model for Estimating the Cost of Equity Capital: The Impact of Real Options of Investment Projects. *Economic Systems* 46 (1), 100874.

3 Modelling of pricing considering the ICAPM

3.1 Modelling of future states of the economy

The FUN is defined by equation (1). The research also reveals a significant relationship between FUN values and future average returns on stock investments (see Chapter 4). Thus, it can be concluded that the state variable driving future returns can be modelled based on the FUN functional values (Urbański and Zarzecki 2022).

$$\begin{aligned}\text{FUN} &= \frac{\text{NUM}}{\text{DEN}} \\ &= \frac{\text{nor}(\text{ROE}) \times \text{nor}(\text{ASB}) \times \text{nor}(\text{APOB}) \times \text{nor}(\text{APNB})}{\text{nor}(\text{ME}) \times \text{nor}(\text{MB})}\end{aligned} \tag{1}$$

where

$$\text{ROE} = F_1 \tag{2}$$

$$\text{ASB} = F_2 = \frac{\left\{\sum_{t=1}^{i}\left[S(Q_t)\right]\right\} / \text{BV}(Q_t)}{\sum_{t=1}^{i}\overline{\text{SBV}(nQ_t)}} \tag{3}$$

$$\text{APOB} = F_3 = \frac{\left\{\sum_{t=1}^{i}\left[\text{PO}(Q_t)\right]\right\} / \text{BV}(Q_t)}{\sum_{t=1}^{i}\overline{\text{POBV}(nQ_t)}} \tag{4}$$

DOI: 10.4324/9781003587330-3

$$\text{APNB} = F_4 = \frac{\left\{\sum_{t=1}^{i}\left[\text{PN}(Q_t)\right]\right\} / \text{BV}(Q_t)}{\sum_{t=1}^{i}\overline{\text{PNBV}(nQ_t)}} \tag{5}$$

$$\text{ME} = F_5 \tag{6}$$

$$\text{MB} = F_6 \tag{7}$$

The variables F_j (j=1,…,6) are transformed to the normalised areas $<a_j; b_j>$ per equation (8):

$$\text{nor}\left(F_j\right) = \left[a_j + \left(b_j - a_j\right) \times \frac{F_j - c_j \times F_j^{\min}}{d_j \times F_j^{\max} - c_j \times F_j^{\min} + e_j}\right] \tag{8}$$

ROE represents the return on book value; $\sum_{t=1}^{i} S(Q_t), \sum_{t=1}^{i} \text{PO}(Q_t)$, and $\sum_{t=1}^{i} \text{PN}(Q_t)$ are the cumulative net sales revenue (S), operating profits (PO), and net profits (PN) from the beginning of the year to the end of the 'i' quarter (Q_i); $\sum_{t=1}^{i}\overline{\text{SBV}(nQ_t)}$, $\sum_{t=1}^{i}\overline{\text{POBV}(nQ_t)}$, and $\sum_{t=1}^{i}\overline{\text{PNBV}(nQ_t)}$ represent the average S/BV, PO/BV, and PN/BV ratios, respectively, accumulated from the start of the year to the end of Q_i over the last n years (where n is assumed to range from 1 to 3, depending on data availability); BV is the book value; ME is the market-to-earnings ratio (for the last four quarters); MB is the market-to-book value ratio; and a_j, b_j, c_j, d_j, and e_j are the variation parameters. In this study, the following parameter values are assumed: $a_j = 1$, $b_j = 2$, $c_j = 1$, $d_j = 1$, and $e_j = 0$.[1]

The first version of the model, MFF2012, considers the structure of past financial results, assuming BV=1, and we denote the FUN functional by FUN2012. The MFF2022 version considers the structure of past financial results in relation to equity capital (BV), and we denote the FUN functional by FUN2022.

The FUN function has a clear economic interpretation and can serve as a criterion for selecting securities for a portfolio. The numerator

(NUM) represents an investor constructing a portfolio of companies with strong fundamentals, while the denominator (DEN) represents an investor selecting undervalued stocks. Therefore, FUN describes a portfolio comprising both fundamentally strong and undervalued stocks (in the case of long-term investments). The attractiveness of the investment increases as the FUN value rises. Chapter 4 discusses the predictive potential of FUN.

3.2 Modelling of equilibrium: Using the author's ICAPM application

The explanatory variables of the proposed model (MFF) are based on the market return (RM), and the variables NUM and DEN, which form the numerator and denominator of FUN. The explanatory variables, X_i, (i=1, 2, 3), are systematic risk factors and are defined as follows:

$$X_1 = E(\text{RM}) - E(\text{RF}) \tag{9a}$$

$$X_2 = E(\text{HMLN}) \tag{9b}$$

$$X_3 = E(\text{LMHD}) \tag{9c}$$

where E(RM) is the expected market return, E(RF) is the expected risk-free return, E(HMLN) (High Minus Low Numerator) is the expected difference in returns between portfolios with the highest and lowest NUM values, LMHD_t (Low Minus High Denominator) is the expected difference in returns between portfolios with the lowest and highest DEN values, as defined by the following relationships:

$$\text{HMLN} = r_{\text{NUM}_{\text{max}}} - r_{\text{NUM}_{\text{min}}}, \tag{10a}$$

$$\text{LMHD} = r_{\text{DEN}_{\text{min}}} - r_{\text{DEN}_{\text{max}}}. \tag{10b}$$

The response variable represents the excess return over the risk-free rate RF for the tested portfolios. The proposed financial model is expressed by equation (11) (Urbański 2012):

$$E(r_i) - E(\text{RF}) = \beta_{iM}\left[E(\text{RM}) - E(\text{RF})\right] + \beta_{i,\text{HMLN}}E(\text{HMLN}) + \beta_{i,\text{LMHD}}E(\text{LMHD}) \tag{11}$$

where i=1, …, m, m is the number of analysed stocks (portfolios).

To compare the accuracy of return descriptions in the context of the ICAPM, the proposed model (11) is compared with the classic FF1993 model. This comparison is achieved through a statistical model consisting of two stages:

1. For the FF1993 model:
1.1. First pass:

$$r_{it} - \text{RF}_t = \beta_{i0} + \beta_{iM}\left[\text{RM}_t - \text{RF}_t\right] + \beta_{i,\text{HML}}\text{HML}_t + \beta_{i,\text{SMB}}\text{SMB}_t + e_{it} \tag{12a}$$

where t=1, ..., T; $\forall$ i=1,…, m.

1.2. Second pass:

$$r_{it} - \text{RF}_t = \gamma_0 + \gamma_M\widehat{\beta_{iM}} + \gamma_{\text{HML}}\widehat{\beta_{i,\text{HML}}} + \gamma_{\text{SMB}}\widehat{\beta_{i,\text{SMB}}} + \varepsilon_{it} \tag{12b}$$

where i=1, …, m; t=1, …, T.

2. For the MFF model:
2.1. First pass:

$$r_{it} - \text{RF}_t = \beta_{i0} + \beta_{iM}\left[\text{RM}_t - \text{RF}_t\right] + \beta_{i,\text{HMLN}}\text{HMLN}_t + \beta_{i,\text{LMHD}}\text{LMHD}_t + e_{it} \tag{13a}$$

where t=1, …, T; $\forall$ i=1,…, m.
2.2. Second pass:

$$r_{it} - \text{RF}_t = \gamma_0 + \gamma_M\widehat{\beta_{iM}} + \gamma_{\text{HMLN}}\widehat{\beta_{i,\text{HMLN}}} + \gamma_{\text{LMHD}}\widehat{\beta_{i,\text{LMHD}}} + \varepsilon_{it} \tag{13b}$$

where i=1, …, m; t=1, …, T.

First-pass parameters (betas - β) represent the components of systematic risk, while the second-pass parameters (gammas - γ) represent the components of risk premiums, derived from the adopted risk factors. The gammas are estimators of expected returns for RM-RF, HML/HMLN and SMB/LMHD—*E*(RM-RF), *E*(HML/HMLN), *E*(SMB/LMHD)—and allow for the assessment of the cost of capital. The cost of capital for the classic FF1993 model is estimated by equation (14a):

$$\widehat{Ccap(\text{FF1993})_i} = E(\text{RF}) + \widehat{\gamma_0} + \widehat{\gamma_M}\widehat{\beta_{iM}^T} + \widehat{\gamma_{\text{HML}}}\widehat{\beta_{i,\text{HML}}^T} + \widehat{\gamma_{\text{SMB}}}\widehat{\beta_{i,\text{SMB}}^T} \tag{14a}$$

The cost of capital for the MFF model is estimated by equation (14b):

$$\widehat{Ccap(\text{MFF})_i} = E(\text{RF}) + \widehat{\gamma_0} + \widehat{\gamma_M}\widehat{\beta_{iM}^T} + \widehat{\gamma_{\text{HMLN}}}\widehat{\beta_{i,\text{HMLN}}^T} + \widehat{\gamma_{\text{LMHD}}}\widehat{\beta_{i,\text{LMHD}}^T} \tag{14b}$$

Here, $\widehat{\beta_{ik}^T}$ represents the systematic risk components estimated via regression for stock *i* relative to the tested model factors *k* (RM-RF, HML, HMLN, SMB, LMHD). *T* is the historical period used for estimating the systematic risk components (see Urbański and Zarzecki 2022, p. 4).

Determining the correctness of the description of returns given the ICAPM requires the following tests:

1. First-pass intercept regression tests.

The first-pass regression intercepts must jointly equal zero for all portfolios:

H0: $\alpha = 0$, where $\alpha = (\alpha_1, \ldots, \alpha_m)'$.

This null hypothesis can be tested using the asymptotic χ^2 distribution based on the Wald statistic (15a) or the Gibbons et al. (1989) test (GRS):

$$\text{W} = \hat{\alpha}' \,\text{Var}[\hat{\alpha}]^{-1}\hat{\alpha}, \sim \chi_m^2 \tag{15a}$$

If the errors e_{it} are iid, the statistic becomes (Cochrane 2001, pp. 217–219):

$$W = \frac{T}{1+E(f_t)' \operatorname{var}[f_t]^{-1} E(f_t)} \hat{\alpha}' \hat{\Sigma}_e^{-1} \hat{\alpha}, \sim \chi_m^2 \tag{15b}$$

The GRS testing statistic is as follows:

$$\mathrm{GRS} = \frac{T}{m} \frac{T-m-k}{T-k-1} \frac{\hat{\alpha}' \hat{\Sigma}_e^{-1} \hat{\alpha}}{1+\bar{\mu}' \Sigma_F^{-1} \bar{\mu}}, \sim F(m, T-m-k) \tag{16}$$

where $\hat{\alpha}$ is the vector of estimated m regression intercepts, $\widehat{\Sigma_e} = \hat{e}'\hat{e}/(T-k-1)$, $\hat{e}$ is the $T \times m$ matrix of residuals, $\bar{\mu}$ is the k–1 vector of mean factor values from T periods, and k is the number of factors.

The GRS statistic follows a non-central F distribution with m and T-m-k degrees of freedom. The non-centrality parameter is given by the relationship: $T \hat{\alpha}' \hat{\Sigma}_e^{-1} \hat{\alpha} (1+(\bar{\mu}' \Sigma_F^{-1} \bar{\mu})^{-1}$. If the null hypothesis holds, the GRS statistic follows a central F distribution with m and T-m-k degrees of freedom (see Gibbons et al. 1989, p. 1146).

2. Systematic risk (β_{ik}) significance test.

Not all beta components are equal to zero:

$$\mathrm{H0}: \beta \neq 0, \text{where. } \beta = (\beta_1, \ldots, \beta_m)' \tag{17}$$

3. The second-pass regression intercepts must satisfy $\gamma_0 = 0$.

4. The risk premium significance test requires that $\gamma_M \neq 0$ and $\gamma_k \neq 0$.

The correctness of the pricing model is verified by ensuring that the estimated residuals are close to zero. A widely used test in ICAPM applications is the ‘correct pricing test’ proposed by Shanken (1985). According to Shanken (1985), this test, based on the Hotelling statistic, serves as a test for the CAPM but can also be applied to the multifactor ICAPM model. The form of the tested model is expressed as (see Shanken 1985, pp. 331, 334 and 343):

$$E(r) = \mathbf{X}\Gamma \tag{18}$$

where for a (k–1) factor model describing m portfolios, $\boldsymbol{X} \equiv [1_m, \hat{\beta}_{m,k-1}]$, betas are estimated using the classic least squares method (CLS), $\Gamma \equiv [\gamma_0, \gamma_1]'$, and γ_1 is a vector containing k–1 components. The gamma vector Γ is estimated via generalised least squares (GLS) after estimating the matrix Σ_e according to the following:

$$\hat{\Gamma} = (\hat{X}' \hat{\Sigma}_e^{-1} \hat{X})^{-1} \hat{X}' \hat{\Sigma}_e^{-1} \bar{r} \tag{19}$$

where $\widehat{\Sigma_e}$ is the sample estimate of the variance and covariance matrix of the random components e_{it} from m regressions of the first pass, obtained from t = 1, ..., T CLS residuals. $\bar{\mathbf{r}}$ is the vector of mean values of the actual returns of the tested time series. The Shanken test statistic defining the total pricing errors of the model (18) is given as follows:

$$Q \equiv T\mathbf{e}'\hat{\Sigma}_e^{-1}\mathbf{e} \tag{20}$$

where $\mathbf{e} \equiv \bar{\mathbf{r}} - \hat{\mathbf{X}}\hat{\Gamma}$, and T is the number of periods. Since the true betas in regression (18) are unknown and must be estimated, the statistic is modified to the following:

$$Q^A \equiv Q / (1 + \widehat{\gamma_1}' \hat{\Sigma}_F^{-1} \widehat{\gamma_1}) \tag{21}$$

where $\hat{\Sigma}_F^{-1}$ is the matrix of variances and covariances of the model factors of the tested sample. The statistic Q^A follows a distribution such as the Hotelling statistic $T^2(m\text{-}k\text{-}1,\ T\text{-}k\text{-}1)$, which converges to $\chi^2(m\text{-}k\text{-}1)$ if $T \to \infty$ (see Hotelling 1933). The T^2 statistic can be transformed to the F statistic. Therefore, the statistic Q^A, following the $F(m\text{-}k\text{-}1,\ T\text{-}m\text{+}1)$ distribution, can be presented as follows (see Shanken 1985, pp. 330, 335, 343–344):

$$Q^A(F) \equiv Q^A(T\text{-}m\text{+}1)/[(T\text{-}k\text{-}1)(m\text{-}k\text{-}1)] \tag{22}$$

The Shanken test can be interpreted as a measure of the 'correctness of pricing' for model (18), with the null hypothesis being that the total pricing errors are zero, as defined by e_{it} (see Shanken 1985, p. 331). Table 3.1 presents the test results from the comparison conducted on the developed market.[2]

Table 3.1 Fama–French (1993) model versus proposed model statistics

Parameter	*Monthly; t=1, …, 204*			*Quarterly; t=1, …, 72*		
	MFF2012 model	*MFF2022 model*	*FF model*	*MFF2012 model*	*MFF2022 model*	*FF model*
γ_0	**0.1324**	**0.1314**	0.0874	0.8690	0.9871	0.2706
t-Stat	**1.6338**	**1.5628**	3.2905	4.6684	4.6656	3.6161
t-Stat(*S*)	**1.6027**	**1.5118**	3.1225	4.3935	4.3875	2.5767
$\gamma_{\mathrm{HMLN/HML}}$	**0.7179**	**0.6971**	**-1.6876**	**1.9841**	**1.6546**	**-3.3598**
t-Stat	**3.2601**	**3.2436**	**-5.3492**	**3.4570**	**2.9405**	**-4.1220**
t-Stat(*S*)	**3.2837**	**3.2657**	**-5.5850**	**3.5901**	**2.9907**	**-6.0172**
$\gamma_{\mathrm{LMHD/SMB}}$	**-0.6477**	**-0.8616**	**-1.0794**	**-1.8320**	**-2.3864**	**-1.8445**
t-Stat	**-3.1511**	**-3.6206**	**-7.0750**	**-2.9800**	**-3.4419**	**-3.6865**
t-Stat(*S*)	**-3.2113**	**-3.7355**	**-8.8064**	**-3.1330**	**-3.6861**	**-3.7015**
$\gamma_{\mathrm{RM-RF}}$	0.0019	0.0073	0.0083	-0.0066	0.0079	-0.0797
t-Stat	0.1186	0.4358	0.4390	-0.1957	0.2185	-1.3820
t-Stat(*S*)	0.1165	0.4221	0.4172	-0.1854	0.2067	-0.9950
GRS	2.2524	**1.6158**	3.3221	**1.4714**	**1.0037**	2.5292
p-value, %	0.12	**3.97**	0.00	**7.91**	**46.49**	0.02
$Q^A(F)$	**1.4420**	**1.3063**	2.4450	**0.7349**	**0.9868**	**1.2738**
p-value, %	**9.04**	**16.20**	0.04	**81.62**	**48.72**	**18.46**
R^2_{LL}, %	**87.80**	**59.17**	**49.63**	**75.78**	**55.18**	**86.90**

FF1993 model: $r_{it} - \mathrm{RF}_t = \gamma_0 + \gamma_M \widehat{\beta_M} + \gamma_{\mathrm{HML}} \widehat{\beta_{\mathrm{HML}}} + \gamma_{\mathrm{SMB}} \widehat{\beta_{\mathrm{SMB}}} + \varepsilon_{it},$

MFF model: $r_{it} - \mathrm{RF}_t = \gamma_0 + \gamma_M \widehat{\beta_M} + \gamma_{\mathrm{HMLN}} \widehat{\beta_{\mathrm{HMLN}}} + \gamma_{\mathrm{LMHD}} \widehat{\beta_{\mathrm{LMHD}}} + \varepsilon_{it},\ i=1, \ldots, 25$

Source: Own research.

Notes: GRS – statistic of multifactor portfolio effective of Gibbons, Ross and Shanken (1989), $Q^A(F)$ – test of correct pricing of Shanken (1985), R^2_{LL} – cross section determination coefficient. *t*-Stat(*S*) – Shanken's (1992) statistic taking into account errors in variables. The factors for developed market: HMLN, HML, LMHD and SMB are calculated using 1726 companies from the S&P 500, S&PCANADA TOPIX 500, and BE 500 indexes. Cases confirming the correct description in the light of ICAPM are marked in bold. Research period: May 2004 to April 2021, 204 months, 72 quarters.

Test results displayed in bold font indicate that the model aligns with the ICAPM; results in standard font suggest that the model does not.

Based on the test results presented in Table 3.1, it can be concluded that the accuracy of return predictions according to the ICAPM for the FF, MFF2012, and MFF2022 models is comparable. These models may be used interchangeably. However, the following distinctions can be made:

1. The state variable influencing future returns in the MFF2012 model is the structure of past financial performance, as modelled by FUN2012.
2. The state variable in the MFF2022 model is the structure of past financial performance relative to equity capital BV, as modelled by FUN2022.
3. The state variable in the FF1993 model is the change in BV/MV.
4. The broader perception of financial results by investors has a direct impact on returns and provides more comprehensive guidance for managers.
5. The information efficiency of the MFF2022 and MFF2012 models is superior.

3.3 Modelling of equilibrium: Sustainability considerations

The contemporary economy faces numerous challenges, particularly those related to evolving approaches to social issues and environmental protection. Ongoing climate change compels governments to implement significant, often radical, measures. These actions influence various aspects of business operations, affecting the financial standing of economic entities and, consequently, the broader market. In light of this, it is essential to consider these factors as influential elements shaping the future state of the economy and financial outcomes.

The concept of sustainable development has gained increasing prominence in recent years, driven by legislative changes introduced by governments and shifts in societal attitudes towards ecology and environmental protection. The growing interest in sustainability and the desire to implement its principles have notably impacted financial markets and their participants.

Sustainable development was first defined in the 1987 World Commission on Environment and Development Report (the Brundtland Report, named after its chair, Gro Harlem Brundtland) as 'meeting current needs without compromising the ability of future generations to meet their own needs' (United Nations 1987). However, numerous definitions exist within the literature, reflecting the concept's evolving nature. This evolution can be traced from the UN Conference in Stockholm (1972) through to the 1987 UN Commission Report, the 'Earth Summit' in Rio de Janeiro (1992), and the 'World Summit on Sustainable Development' in Johannesburg (2002). In recent years, governments and international organisations have particularly focused on combating climate change. This has become a global initiative, with both developed and developing nations taking action. Key developments include the United Nations' 2030 Agenda for Sustainable Development (Sustainable Development Goals), adopted by 193 member states, the European Commission's European Green Deal (2019), and China's 14th Five-Year Plan (2021–2025) which includes a new development strategy for its circular economy. The United States has also committed to achieving net-zero greenhouse gas emissions by 2050 under its Long-Term Strategy (The Long-Term Strategy of the United States Pathways to Net-Zero Greenhouse Gas Emissions by 2050).

However, it is crucial to examine what sustainable development truly entails and how it influences economic activity and, by extension, the market. In the context of business operations, sustainable development entails conducting activities in a manner that does not compromise the ability of future generations to meet their needs. This is achieved by balancing three key aspects: environmental, social, and economic (ESG) factors.

The economic dimension encompasses fundamental tasks of business, such as creating value for shareholders, increasing stock prices, generating profits, and expanding market share. It involves the allocation of limited resources in a manner that ensures equal opportunities for future generations while securing the long-term viability of the enterprise. Activities in this area include dividend policies, methods of capital acquisition, debt management, research and development investments, wage structures, public liabilities, economic policies, corruption prevention, and litigation management (Roszkowska 2011).

The social dimension concerns activities that benefit society. Every business operates within a broader social context, which significantly influences its success or failure. No organisation can function in isolation from the community, and the well-being of an organisation is closely linked to the welfare of society as a whole. Therefore, the primary goal of any organisation should be to promote well-being and equal opportunities for all, irrespective of socio-economic background. This can be achieved through various means, including alleviating hunger and poverty, improving healthcare access, reducing child mortality, enhancing gender equality, providing access to education, and supporting environmental protection (Roszkowska 2011).

The environmental dimension focuses on the management of natural resources. Sustainable use of resources aims to minimise, or ideally eliminate, adverse effects on biodiversity. This includes the responsible management of non-renewable resources such as oil, natural gas, gold, and silver, and the promotion of renewable resources like solar energy and bioenergy. Efforts to minimise negative societal impacts can be realised through actions such as reducing emissions of harmful gases (e.g., SO_2, NO_x), minimising industrial waste and wastewater production, and preventing water pollution. These goals can be supported by eco-friendly investments, such as advanced technologies to reduce emissions, recycling initiatives, and the adoption of renewable energy sources like wind and solar power (Roszkowska 2011).

While each of these dimensions is vital, their balance and interaction are what enable the maximisation of sustainable development outcomes. The concept of sustainable development closely aligns with that of corporate social responsibility (CSR). However, sustainable development is broader in scope than CSR, as it encompasses all entities, not just businesses. Despite this, the principles of sustainable development are highly consistent with the objectives of social responsibility.

The impact of companies' involvement in socially responsible activities and sustainable development issues has been extensively studied. However, the findings are inconclusive, largely due to varying approaches in defining the measures of socially responsible activities consistent with sustainable development principles. Several studies, including those by Moskowitz (1972), Bragdon and Martin (1972), Bowman and Haire (1975), Belkaoui (1976), Spicer (1978), Anderson and Frankle (1980), Lener and Fryxell (1988), Simerly (1995), Hart and Ahuja (1996), Waddock and Graves (1997), Preston and O'Bannon (1997), Johnson and Greening (1999), Orlitzky et al. (2003), Ngwakwe (2008), Godfrey et al. (2009), Cellier and Chollet (2011), Cheng et al. (2014), Reverte (2012), Endrikat et al. (2014), Sun and Rakhman (2013), and Gregory et al. (2014) have demonstrated a positive relationship between financial performance and socially responsible activities.

Conversely, studies by Fogler and Nutt (1975), Vance (1975), Galbreath (2006), Di Donato and Izzo (2012), and Oikonomou et al. (2012) have shown a negative relationship. Other studies, such as those by Buehler and Shetty (1976), Fry and Hock (1976), Alexander and Buchholz (1978), Ingram (1978), Abbott and Monsen (1979), Aupperle et al. (1985), McWilliams and Siegel (2000), Brine et al. (2006), Fiori et al. (2007) have found no significant relationship between corporate social performance (CSP) (i.e. in ESG) and corporate financial performance (CFP).

Inconsistent results are also reported by Belkaoui and Karpik (1989), Blackburn et al. (1994), Luo and Bhattacharya (2006), Mittal et al. (2008), Inoue and Lee (2011), Tang et al. (2012), Yusoff et al. (2013), Dobrescu (2013), Patari et al. (2014), and Wang et al. (2016).

The relationship between CSP and CFP is crucial, both for understanding how sustainable development activities might influence future economic conditions and for assessing their impact on financial outcomes. A comprehensive review of the literature indicates that this issue has been examined for over 50 years. However, the broad scope of CSR and associated social initiatives complicates the development of a single, effective measure that captures a company's social achievements. The absence of such a measure impedes efforts to clearly demonstrate a positive or negative relationship between social and financial performance. Although a variety of methods have been employed to define social performance variables, it appears impossible to fully encapsulate all CSR and sustainable development achievements in a single metric.

The lack of universal measurement systems means that studies examining the relationship between CSP and CFP often yield diverse results. Variability may arise from issues such as the choice of variables for both social and financial performance, as well as differences in research methodology. Furthermore, variations in research periods, geographical regions, and firm sizes likely contribute to the differences observed. Existing studies report mixed findings: some indicate a positive relationship, others show a negative or no relationship, and a few offer conflicting results—where financial performance is linked both positively and negatively with social performance. Despite these inconsistencies, it remains worthwhile to incorporate CSR factors into financial models.

As previously noted, defining a single measure for CSR and sustainable development remains challenging. However, adopting ratings developed by firms such as MSCI, Bloomberg, Thomson Reuters, RobecoSAM, or Sustainalytics seems a plausible solution. These ratings aggregate various ESG factors into a synthetic measure, frequently employed in research (e.g., Cheng et al. 2014; Gregory et al. 2014; Inoue and Lee 2011; Johnson and Greening 1999; Oikonomou et al. 2012; Patari et al. 2014; Reverte 2012; Sun and Rakhman 2013; Tang et al. 2012; Waddock and Graves 1997; Wang et al. 2016). Key ratings of this type include Thomson Reuters ESG scores (formerly ASSETS4 ESG), LSEG ESG Scores (formerly Refinitiv ESG), and MSCI KLD.

Within the literature, some scholars propose incorporating the ESG factor as a risk variable. Despite the varied results, most studies suggest a statistically significant link between social (CSP/ESG) and financial performance (CFP). This supports the notion that ESG can be considered a risk factor in multifactor models, such as the CAPM.

Reverte (2012) identifies a negative relationship between the quality of CSR reporting and the cost of equity for Spanish companies listed on the IBEX35, particularly for firms in environmentally sensitive industries. CSR reporting, as Reverte notes, serves as a communication tool that reduces information asymmetry between managers and investors, enabling more accurate company pricing. Reverte extends Fama and French's three-factor model by incorporating a CSR reporting quality factor. The extended model is formulated as follows:

$$\begin{aligned} \mathrm{CC}_{it} &= \beta_0 + \beta_1 * BETA_{it} + \beta_2 * MB_{it} + \beta_3 * SIZE_{it} \\ &\quad + \beta_4 * CSR\_SCORE_{it} + \varepsilon_{it} \end{aligned} \tag{23}$$

where:

CC_{it} is the cost of equity capital for firm i at time t, as in $\mathrm{CC}_i = \sqrt{\frac{\mathrm{eps}_{i,t} - \mathrm{eps}_{i,t+1}}{P_{o,i}}}$, where $\mathrm{eps}_{i,t}$ and $\mathrm{eps}_{i,t+1}$ are the analysts'

consensus forecasts of earnings per share for firm *i* for one and two years ahead, respectively, as of the end of year *t*, and $P_{o,i}$ is stock market price of firm *i*'s shares at the forecast date (end of year *t*);
BETA_{it} is the market model beta for firm *i* at time *t* (estimated over the 60 months prior to a firm-year observation fiscal year end with the market model);
MB_{it} is the fiscal year-end market value of equity divided by the fiscal year-end book value of equity for firm *i* at time *t*;
SIZE_{it} is the natural log of the fiscal year-end market value of equity for firm *i* at time *t*;
CSR_SCORE_{it} is the corporate CSR rating, where a higher value reflects better CSR reporting quality.
The CSR_SCORE_{it} metric is the CSR disclosure score developed by the Observatory on CSR, published for the years 2003–2008.

Zhou (2022) modifies the Fama and French three-factor model by introducing an ESG factor, termed **SMU** (Sustainable minus Unsustainable). This factor is defined as the return spread between the top 30% high-ESG (Sustainable, S) group and the bottom 30% low-ESG (Unsustainable, U) group, based on the Wind ESG Rating. The proposed model is expressed as:

$$R_{it} - R_{ft} = \alpha_{it} + \beta_1 \left(R_{Mt} - R_{ft}\right) + \beta_2 \text{SMB}_t + \beta_3 \text{HML}_t + \beta_4 \text{SMU}_t + \epsilon_{it} \tag{24}$$

where:
R_{it} is the monthly return of portfolio *i* at time *t*;
R_{ft} is the risk-free rate of return at time *t*;
R_{Mt} is the total market portfolio return at time *t*;
SMB_t is the size premium (Small minus Big) at time *t*;
HML_t is the value premium (High minus Low) at time *t*;
SMU_t is the ESG premium (SMU) at time *t*;
$\beta_{1,2,3,4}$ represent the factor coefficients;
α_{it} is the alpha of portfolio *i* at time *t*.

Based on a study of 3,430 Chinese companies, the ESG 4-factor model (market premium, SMB, HML, SMU) slightly outperforms the Fama and French three-factor model. The ESG factor plays a significant role in predicting returns, suggesting its importance in investment decision-making. Zhou also highlights that 'investors could earn higher returns and mitigate downside risks by investing in high-ESG stocks' (Zhou 2022).

Mulialim and Madyan (2023) also propose a modification to the Fama and French three-factor model, adding an ESG factor based on Thomson Reuters ESG scores. Their model is expressed as:

$$R_i - R_f = \alpha + \beta\left(R_m - R_f\right) + \beta \mathrm{SMB} + \beta \mathrm{HML}_{\mathrm{bme}} + \beta \mathrm{HML}_{\mathrm{esg}} + \epsilon \quad (25)$$

where:

R_i is the realised stock return *i* period *t*;
R_f is the risk-free asset return period *t*;
R_m is the market return period *t*;
α is a constant;
β is the sensitivity of stock *i* to each factor;
SMB is the return small firm minus the big firm;
$\mathrm{HML}_{\mathrm{bme}}$ is the return high book-to-market Equity minus low-book-to-market Equity;
$\mathrm{HML}_{\mathrm{esg}}$ is the return high score ESG equity minus low score ESG equity ($\mathrm{HML}_{\mathrm{esg}} = \dfrac{(SH + BH) - (SL + BL)}{2}$, where *SL* is the return of companies with small (*S*) and low ESG Scores (*L*); *SH* is the return of companies with small (*S*) and high ESG Scores (*H*); *BL* is the portfolio of companies with big (*B*) and low ESG Scores (*L*); and *BH* is the company portfolio with big (*B*) and has a High ESG Scores (*H*));
ϵ is the error.

Based on data from companies listed in Indonesia's LQ45 index (2015–2019), Mulialim and Madyan (2023) find that their four-factor ESG model better explains excess returns compared to the Fama and French three-factor model. Their results indicate that 'high-ESG companies tend to have lower risk than low-ESG companies, meaning investors require higher returns for low-ESG companies' (Mulialim and Madyan 2023).

Mio et al. (2023) use three fixed-effects panel regression models to analyse the cost of equity (COE):

Model 1:

$$\text{COE}_{i,t} = \beta_1 \text{ESG}_{i,t} + \text{ControlVariables} + \alpha_i + \varepsilon_{i,t} \tag{26}$$

Model 2:

$$\begin{aligned}\text{COE}_{i,t} = {} & \beta_1 \text{ENV}_{i,t} + \beta_2 \text{SOC}_{i,t} + \beta_3 \text{GOV}_{i,t} \\ & + \text{ControlVariables} + \alpha_i + \varepsilon_{i,t}\end{aligned} \tag{27}$$

Model 3:

$$\begin{aligned}\text{COE}_{i,t} = {} & \beta_1 \text{RESOURCE}_{i,t} + \beta_2 \text{EMISSION}_{i,t} \\ & + \beta_3 \text{INNOV}_{i,t} + \beta_4 \text{WORKFORCE}_{i,t} \\ & + \beta_5 \text{HR}_{i,t} + \beta_6 \text{COMMUNITY}_{i,t} \\ & + \beta_7 \text{PROD}_{i,t} + \beta_8 \text{MANAG}_{i,t} \\ & + \beta_9 \text{SHARE}_{i,t} + \beta_{10} \text{CSR}_{i,t} \\ & + \text{ControlVariables} + \alpha_i + \varepsilon_{i,t}\end{aligned} \tag{28}$$

where:

$\text{COE}_{i,t}$ is the cost of equity for firm *i* at time *t*, is calculated using the CAPM;

$\text{ESG}_{i,t}$ is the Refinitiv ESG score for firm *i* at time *t*;

$\text{ENV}_{i,t}$ is the Refinitiv Environment score for firm *i* at time *t*;

$\text{SOC}_{i,t}$ is the Refinitiv Social score for firm *i* at time *t*;

$\text{GOV}_{i,t}$ is the Refinitiv Governance score for firm *i* at time *t*;

$\text{RESOURCE}_{i,t}$ is the resource use category score (Refinitiv), which, for firm *i* at time *t*, reflects the performance and capacity to reduce the use of materials, energy, or water and find more eco-efficient solutions by improving supply chain management;

$\text{EMISSION}_{i,t}$ is the emission category score (Refinitiv), which, for firm *i* at time *t*, measures the commitment and effectiveness towards reducing environmental emissions in the production and operational processes;

$\text{INNOV}_{i,t}$ is the environmental innovation category score (Refinitiv), which, for firm *i* at time *t*, reflects the capacity to reduce the environmental costs and burdens for its customers, thereby creating new market opportunities through new environmental technologies and processes or eco-designed products;

$\text{WORKFORCE}_{i,t}$ is the workforce category score (Refinitiv), which, for firm *i* at time *t*, measures the effectiveness towards job satisfaction, healthy and safe workplace, maintaining diversity and equal opportunities, and development opportunities for its workforce;

$\text{HR}_{i,t}$ is the human rights category score (Refinitiv), which, for firm *i* at time *t*, measures the effectiveness towards respecting the fundamental human rights conventions;

$\text{COMMUNITY}_{i,t}$ is the community category score (Refinitiv), which, for firm *i* at time *t*, measures the commitment towards being a good citizen, protecting public health, and respecting business ethics;

$\text{PROD}_{i,t}$ is the product responsibility category score (Refinitiv), which, for firm *i* at time *t*, reflects the capacity to produce quality goods and services integrating the customer's health and safety, integrity, and data privacy;

$\text{MANAG}_{i,t}$ is the management category score (Refinitiv), which, for firm *i* at time *t*, measures the commitment and effectiveness towards following best practice corporate governance principles;

$\text{SHARE}_{i,t}$ is the shareholders category score (Refinitiv), which, for firm *i* at time *t*, measures the effectiveness towards equal treatment of shareholders and the use of anti-takeover devices;

$\text{CSR}_{i,t}$ is the CSR strategy category score (Refinitiv), which, for firm *i* at time *t*, reflects the practices to communicate and integrate economic (financial), social, and environmental dimensions into the day-today decision-making processes;

ControlVariables include the logarithm of total assets (*SIZE*), ratio of total debt to book value of equity (*LEV*), ratio of the book value of equity to the market value of equity (*BTM*); return on assets (*ROA*), standard deviation of one-year-ahead analyst forecasts of earnings per share (*DISPERSION*), and the number of unique analysts issuing earnings per share forecasts (*NUM*) for firm *i* at time *t*.

ESG data were collected from the Refinitiv ESG database. Mio et al. (2023) analysed a sample of 273 firm-year observations from 60 companies listed in the S&P 500 and EuroStoxx 600 indices between 2017 and 2021. They found a positive relationship between the overall ESG score and the cost of equity, although further analysis revealed that only a few ESG factors significantly influence risk perception.

Given these findings, it is possible to modify the MFF2012 model to include an ESG factor. Building on Zhou's (2022) proposal for the FF1993 model, the modified version is expressed as:

$$r_{it} - \mathrm{RF}_t = \beta_{i0} + \beta_{iM}\left[\mathrm{RM}_t - \mathrm{RF}_t\right] + \beta_{i,\mathrm{HMLN}}\mathrm{HMLN}_t + \beta_{i,\mathrm{LMHD}}\mathrm{LMHD}_t + \beta_{i,\mathrm{SMU}}\mathrm{SMU}_t + e_{it} \tag{29}$$

where:

SMU_t is the ESG Premium (SMU) at time t, as in $\mathrm{SMU}_t = r_{\mathrm{ESG_{MAX}}} - r_{\mathrm{ESG_{MIN}}}$, defined as the return spread between the top 30% high-ESG (Sustainable, S) group and the bottom 30% low-ESG (Unsustainable, U) group; and $\beta_{i,\mathrm{SMU}}$ is the component of systematic risk given SMU factors.

To assess ESG performance, the literature frequently uses ESG/CSR rankings from reputable data providers. Examples include MSCI KLD ratings, Bloomberg ESG Scores, LSEG ESG Scores, RobecoSAM's ESG Rating Business, and Sustainalytics' Company ESG Risk Ratings. For instance, LSEG ESG Scores, covering over 90% of the global market capitalisation (over 16,000 companies globally), are based on more than 870 ESG metrics with data dating back to 2002 (LSEG 2024). Similarly, Bloomberg ESG Scores incorporate over 120 data points across environmental, social, and governance dimensions (www.esg-advising.com).

3.4 Estimation of pricing models

In general, pricing problems may be nonlinear, necessitating nonlinear estimation methods such as Newton-Raphson or Gauss-Newton, along with their various modifications (Maddala 2006, pp. 444–447). For linear models, methods such as least squares, maximum likelihood, and the generalised method of moments may be employed. However, linear regression relies on several assumptions, many of which are difficult to satisfy in practice. The main issues that hinder the accurate estimation of regression parameters include:

- mutual correlation of explanatory variables (called collinearity),
- randomness of explanatory variables,
- heterogeneity of variance of random components and dependence of random components among themselves, $E(\boldsymbol{ee}') \neq \sigma^2\mathbf{I}$,
- heteroscedasticity and autocorrelation phenomena of random components,
- inaccurate estimation of explanatory variables of second-pass regression constituting estimated parameters of first-pass regression, called errors in variables.

Among these, heteroscedasticity and autocorrelation are typically the most significant. Miller and Scholes (1972) identified heteroscedasticity in the random components of the pricing model but found no relationship between this phenomenon and higher intercept values or lower slopes. Instead, heteroscedasticity tends to bias parameter estimates in the opposite direction. The autocorrelation of the random components is dependent on the selection of factors and may significantly affect the parameter estimates from the first pass of time-series regressions. In cross-sectional time-series estimation based on panel data, it can be assumed that autocorrelation of pricing errors does not exist, as explanatory variables (betas) are constant across periods, while the dependent variable, return, is assumed to be random (see Cochrane 2001, p. 247).

The impact of heteroscedasticity and autocorrelation can be accounted for by using the GLS method, alongside White or Newey-West estimators to compute the variance and covariance matrices of regression parameters (Greene 2003).

Miller and Scholes (1972) also observed that while returns generally follow an approximately normal distribution, they are typically right-skewed. This skewness implies that cross-sectional regression may show a relationship between residual risk and returns, even when no such relationship exists. This issue can be mitigated by appropriately selecting the investment period and grouping stocks into portfolios. Returns over short periods (e.g., weekly or daily) tend to deviate significantly from normality, while long-term returns (annual or longer) for individual stocks are typically right-skewed. This is because returns are bounded below, and over long periods, the likelihood of price increases greater than 100% rises. By grouping stocks into portfolios, the return distributions for these portfolios will approximate normality.

Another critical issue in capital market equilibrium modelling is the effect of errors in variable specification. Miller and Scholes (1972) argue that errors in estimating beta lead to an underestimation of the parameter adjacent to beta in second-pass regression and an overestimation of the intercept. Moreover, errors in measuring beta have important consequences. If true beta is positively correlated with the variance of the random component for a given security, the variance will partially substitute for the true beta, and returns will become positively correlated with residual risk. Although the return is not dependent on the random component's variance, a statistical relationship may emerge in cross-sectional regressions. The influence of residual risk can be reduced, and beta estimation improved, by grouping stocks into portfolios.

Errors in estimating actual betas in the first pass can be addressed by adjusting the standard errors of the gamma parameters estimated in the second pass. Shanken (1992, p. 13) proposes a corrected estimator for the variance-covariance matrix of the parameters, given by:

$$\widehat{\Sigma_{\Gamma}^{\mathrm{adj}}} = (1+c)(\widehat{\Sigma_{\Gamma}} - \widehat{\Sigma_{F}^{*}}) + \widehat{\Sigma_{F}^{*}} \tag{30}$$

where $\widehat{\Sigma_{\Gamma}}$ is the matrix of variances and covariances of gamma parameters estimated from the sample, and $\widehat{\Sigma_{F}^{*}}$ is the matrix of variances and covariances of the model factors, divided by the number of periods, T. The scalar c is defined as:

$$c = \hat{\Gamma}' \widehat{\Sigma_{F}^{-1}} \hat{\Gamma} \tag{31}$$

The corrected t-statistic for the estimated second-pass gamma parameters is:

$$\mathrm{SH}t = \frac{\hat{\Gamma}}{[(\hat{\Sigma}_{\Gamma}^{\mathrm{adj}})_{kk}]^{1/2}} \tag{32}$$

where $(\hat{\Sigma}_{\Gamma}^{\mathrm{adj}})_{kk}$ is the k-th element of the main diagonal of the matrix $\hat{\Sigma}_{\Gamma}^{\mathrm{adj}}$.

3.5 Efficient market hypotheses: Discretisation problems

Considering FF1995 and the considerations outlined above, the investment portfolio of a representative investor should be constructed based on the structure of past long-term financial outcomes relative to equity capital. To this end, portfolio construction can be guided by the maximisation of FUN. As previously noted, all known and unknown investment strategies may be based on FUN. Forming an investment portfolio using FUN, as in the case of constructing BV/MV portfolios in the FF1993 model, is a sufficient condition for returns to align with the ICAPM. However, this is not a necessary condition. Another portfolio, formed using a different functional form, *FUN_x*, could yield similarly good or better results. This strategy aims to more accurately model past financial outcomes and generate future returns in accordance with the ICAPM, at a higher level of significance. Consequently, if a representative investor recognises that future returns are determined by the past structure of financial results, they will seek to identify a known or unknown *FUN_x*, that best models the past structure of profits in relation to the company's equity.[3]

If the representative investor is dominant in the market (assuming rational decision-making), no other investment strategy can outperform the market, and the market is efficient. Thus, market efficiency tests can be reduced to examining whether a representative investor constructs portfolios whose returns are consistent with the ICAPM. This research can proceed in two directions:

Direction A – Portfolios formed based on the structure of past financial results either generate or do not generate significantly higher returns than the market portfolio. According to Fama's Efficient Markets Hypothesis (Fama 1970) and the findings of Malkiel (2003, 2016), a market is efficient if no investment strategy outperforms the market.

Direction B – This approach involves multifactor efficiency tests of the portfolios formed (Chou and Zhou 2006). It tests the correctness of the chosen pricing model in the context of the ICAPM, using tests such as the Wald test, Gibbons et al. (1989) test, and correct pricing tests (Roll 1985; Shanken 1985).

This study focuses solely on **Direction A**.

Based on the preceding considerations, we hypothesise the following conjectures:

Conjecture 1:

The average returns generated by the selected portfolios formed on FUN values differ from the average returns of the portfolio modelled with the benchmark index of the analysed market.

Conjecture 2:

The Sharpe ratios (SRs) of the selected portfolios formed on FUN values differ from the SR of the portfolio modelled with the benchmark index of the analysed market.

Conjecture 3:

The differences between the average returns generated by FUN and the benchmark returns are attributable to differences in portfolio capitalisation. Specifically, these differences are due to the inclusion of small-cap companies in FUN-formed portfolios, compared to the presence of large-cap companies in the benchmark portfolio.

If Conjectures 1 and 2 hold true, it can be inferred that the tested market is not efficient. Conversely, if Conjectures 1 and 2 are not supported, there is no basis for concluding that the market is inefficient.

Confirmation of Conjecture 3 would indicate that the validity or invalidity of Conjectures 1 and 2 is linked to the capitalisation structure of the FUN and benchmark portfolios.

To test the validity of these conjectures, we estimate the returns and SRs of the selected portfolios formed on FUN values. Details of the research scope are presented in Chapter 4.

Notes

1 For the chosen variation parameter values, all indices F_j are transposed onto <1; 2> intervals.

2 We define developed markets following Kenneth R. French's classification (see: https://mba.tuck.dartmouth.edu/pages/faculty/ken.french/Data_Library/f-f_5developed.html) as those in the EU, US, Japan, and Canada. The developed market is selected to compare the accuracy of return descriptions (for the three pricing applications studied) in the broadest market for which data is available. For the classic FF model, the HML and SMB factors are sourced from the FF website.

3 Similarly, for a CAPM investor, all investment strategies involving risky assets (assuming the presence of a risk-free asset) are determined by a portfolio located on the tangent of the Capital Market Line and the Markowitz minimum risk set.

References

Abbott, W.F., & Monsen, R.J. (1979). On the Measurement of Corporate Social Responsibility: Self-Reported Disclosures as a Method of Measuring

Corporate Social Involvement. *Academy of Management Journal* 22 (3), 501–515.

Alexander, G.J., & Buchholz, R.A. (1978). Corporate Social Responsibility and Stock Market Performance. *Academy of Management Journal* 21 (3), 479–486.

Anderson, J.C., & Frankle, A.W. (1980). Voluntary Social Reporting: As Iso-Beta Portfolio Analysis. *Accounting Review* LV (3), 468–479.

Aupperle, K.E., Carroll, A.B., & Hatfield, J.D. (1985). An Empirical Examination of the Relationship Between Corporate Social Responsibility and Profitability. *Academy of Management Journal* 28 (2), 446–463.

Belkaoui, A. (1976). The Impact of the Disclosure of the Environmental Effects of Organizational Behavior on the Market. *Financial Management* 5 (4), 26–31.

Belkaoui, A., & Karpik, P. (1989). Determinants of the Corporate Decision to Disclose Social Information. *Accounting, Auditing and Accountability Journal* 2 (1), 36–51.

Blackburn, V., Doran, M., & Shrader, C.B. (1994). Investigating the Dimensions of Social Responsibility and the Consequences for Corporate Financial Performance. *Journal of Managerial Issues* 6 (2, Summer 1994), 195–212.

Bowman, E., & Haire, M. (1975). A Strategic Posture Toward Corporate Social Responsibility. *California Management Review* XVIII (2), 49–58.

Bragdon, J.H., & Marlin, J.A. (1972). Is Pollution Profitable? *Risk Management* 19 (4), 9–18.

Brine, M., Brown, R., & Hackett, G. (2006). Corporate Social Responsibility and Financial Performance in the Australian Context. *Economic Round-up, Autumn* 2007, 47–58.

Buehler, V.M., & Shetty, Y.K. (1976). Managerial Response to Social Responsibility Challenge. *Academy of Management Journal* 19 (1), 66–78.

Cellier, A., & Chollet, P. (2011). The Impact of Corporate Social Responsibility Rating Announcements on European Stock Prices. *International Conference of the French Finance Association* (AFFI), May 11-13, 2011.

Cheng, B., Ioannou, I., & Serafeim, G. (2014). Corporate Social Responsibility and Access to Finance. *Strategic Management Journal* 35, 1–23.

Chou, P.-H., & Zhou, G. (2006). Using Bootstrap to Test Portfolio Efficiency. *Annals of Economics and Finance* 7 (2), 217–249. https://doi.org/10.54254/2754-1169/3/2022892

Cochrane, J. (2001). *Asset Pricing*. Princeton, NJ: Princeton University Press.

Di Donato, F., & Izzo, M.F. (2012). The Relation between Corporate Social Responsibility and Stock Prices: An Analysis of the Italian Listed Companies.https://papers.ssrn.com/sol3/Delivery.cfm/SSRN_ID1986324_code907333.pdf?abstractid=1986324&mirid=1 (Accessed October 30, 2017).

Dobrescu, D. (2013). The Impact of Corporate Social Responsibility on Corporate Value. *The USV Annals of Economics and Public Administration* 13 (2), 91–101.

Endrikat, J., Guenther, E., & Hoppe, H. (2014). Making Sense of Conflicting Empirical Findings: A Meta-Analytic Review of the Relationship Between Corporate Environmental and Financial Performance. *European Management Journal* 32, 735–751.

European Commission (2019). *Communication from the Commission to the European Parliament, the Council, the European Economic and Social Committee and the Committee of the Regions*. 11.12.2019 COM(2019) 640 final. Brussels: The European Green Deal, Brussels.

Fama, E.F. (1970). Efficient Capital Markets: A Review of Theory and Empirical Work. *Journal of Finance* 25 (2), 383–417.

Fama, E.F., & French, K.R. (1993). Common Risk Factors in the Returns on Stocks and Bonds. *Journal of Financial Economics* 33, 3–56.

Fama, E.F., & French, K.R. (1995). Size and Book-to-Market Factors in Earnings and Returns. *Journal of Finance* 50 (1), 131–155.

Fiori, G., di Donato, F., & Izzo, M.F. (2007). Corporate Social Responsibility and Firms Performance – An Analysis on Italian Listed Companies. https://papers.ssrn.com/sol3/papers.cfm?abstract_id=1032851 (Accessed November 11, 2017).

Fogler, H.R., & Nutt, F. (1975). A Note on Social Responsibility and Stock Valuation. *Academy of Management Journal* 18 (1), 155–160.

Fry, F., & Hock, R. (1976). Who Claims Corporate Responsibility? The Biggest and the Worst. *Business and Society Review* 18 (18), 62–65.

Galbreath, J. (2006). Does Primary Stakeholder Management Positively Affect the Bottom Line? Some Evidence from Australia. *Management Decision* 44 (8), 1106–1121.

Gibbons, M.R., Ross, S.A., & Shanken, J. (1989). A Test of the Efficiency of a Given Portfolio. *Econometrica* 57 (5), 1121–1152.

Godfrey, P.C., Merrill, C.B., & Hansen, J.M. (2009). The Relationship Between Corporate Social Responsibility and Shareholder Value: An Empirical Test of the Risk Management Hypothesis. *Strategic Management Journal* 30 (4), 425–445.

Greene, W.H. (2003). *Econometric Analysis*. Upper Saddle River, NJ: Prentice Hall.

Gregory, A., Tharyan, R., & Whittaker, J. (2014). Corporate Social Responsibility and Firm Value: Disaggregating the Effects on Cash Flow, Risk and Growth. *Journal of Business Ethics* 124 (4), 633–657.

Hart, S.L., & Ahuja, G. (1996). Does it Pat to be Green? An Empirical Examination of the Relationship Between Emission Reduction and Firm Performance. *Business Strategy and the Environment* 5, 30–37.

Hotelling, H. (1933). Analysis of a Complex of Statistical Variables into Principal Components. *Journal of Educational Psychology* 24, 417-441.

Ingram, R. (1978). An Investigation of the Information Content of (Certain) Social Responsibility Disclosures. *Journal of Accounting Research* 16 (2), 270–285.

Inoue, Y., & Lee, S. (2011). Effects of Different Dimensions of Corporate Social Responsibility on Corporate Financial Performance in Tourism-Related Industries. *Tourism Management* 32, 790–804.

Johnson, R.A., & Greening, D.W. (1999). The Effects of Corporate Governance and Institutional Ownership Types on Corporate Social Performance. *Academy of Management Journal* 42 (5), 564–576.

Lener, L.D., & Fryxell, G.E. (1988). An Empirical Study of the Predictors of Corporate Social Performance: A Multi-Dimensional Analysis. *Journal of Business Ethics* 7 (12), 951–959.

LSEG (2024). *Environmental, social and governance scores from LSEG.* October 2024. LSEG Data & Analytics. https://www.lseg.com/content/dam/data-analytics/en_us/documents/methodology/lseg-esg-scores-methodology.pdf?ref=zoya-blog (Accessed March 25, 2025).

Luo, X., & Bhattacharya, C.B. (2006). Corporate Social Responsibility, Customer Satisfaction, and Market Value. *Journal of Marketing* 70, 1–18.

Maddala, G.S. (2006). *Introduction to Econometrics*. Chichester: Wiley.

Malkiel, B.G. (2003). The Efficient Market Hypothesis and Its Critics. *Journal of Economic Perspective* 17 (1), 59–82.

Malkiel, B.G. (2016). *A Random Walk Down Wall Street: The Time-Tested Strategy for Successful Investing*. New York: W.W. Norton.

McWilliams, A., & Siegel, D. (2000). Corporate Social Responsibility and Financial Performance: Correlation or Misspecification? *Strategic Management Journal* 21, 603–609.

Miller, M.H., & Scholes M. (1972). Rate of Return in Relation to Risk: A Re-Examination of Some Recent Findings. In M.C. Jensen (ed.), *Studies in the Theory of Capital Markets*. New York: Praeger.

Mio, C., Fasan, M., & Scarpa, F. (2023). Materiality Investor Perspectives on Utilities' ESG Performance. An Empirical Analysis of ESG Factors and Cost of Equity. *Utilities Policy* 82, 101555.

Mittal, R.K., Sinha, N., & Singh, A. (2008). An Analysis of Linkage Between Economic Value Added and Corporate Social Responsibility. *Management Decision* 46 (9), 1437–1443.

Moskowitz, M. (1972). Choosing Socially Responsible Stocks. *Business and Society Review* 1, 71–75.

Mulialim, C., & Madyan, M. (2023). How Does ESG Explain Excess Returns in Emerging Market? An Asset-Pricing Approach. *Journal of Theoretical and Applied Management* 16 (2), 280–293.

Ngwakwe, C.C. (2008). Environmental Responsibility and Firm Performance: Evidence from Nigeria. *International Journal of Social, Human Science and Engineering* 2 (10), 6–13.

Oikonomou, I., Brooks, C., & Pavelin, S. (2012). The Impact of Corporate Social Performance on Financial Risk and Utility: A Longitudinal Analysis. *Financial Management* 41 (2), 483–515.

Orlitzky, M., Schmidt, F.L., & Rynes, S.L. (2003). Corporate Social Performance and Financial Performance: A Meta-analysis. *Organization Studies* 24 (3), 403–441.

Patari, S., Arminen, H., Tuppura, A., & Jantunen, A. (2014). Competitive and Responsible? The Relationship Between Corporate Social and Financial Performance in the Energy Sector. *Renewable and Sustainable Energy Reviews* 37, 142–154.

Preston, L.E., & O'Bannon, D.P. (1997). The Corporate Social-Financial Performance Relationship. A Typology and Analysis. *Business and Society* 36 (4), 419–429.

Reverte, C. (2012). The Impact of Better Corporate Social Responsibility Disclosure on the Cost of Equity Capital. *Corporate Social Responsibility and Environmental Management* 19, 253–272.

Roll, R. (1985). A Note on the Geometry of Shanken CSR T^2 Test for Mean/Variance Efficiency. *Journal of Financial Economics* 14, 349–357.

Roszkowska, P. (2011). *Rewolucja w raportowaniu biznesowym. Interesariusze, konkurencyjność, społeczna odpowiedzialność.* Warsaw (Poland): Difin. Warsaw.

Shanken, J. (1985). Multivariate Tests of the Zero-Beta CAPM. *Journal of Financial Economics* 14 (3), 327–348.

Simerly, R.L. (1995). Institutional, Ownership, Corporate Social Performance, and Firms' Financial Performance. *Psychological Reports* 77, 515–525.

Spicer, B.H. (1978). Investors, Corporate Social Performance and Information Disclosure: An Empirical Study. *The Accounting Review* LIII (1), 94–111.

Sun, L., & Rakhman, F. (2013). CFO Financial Expertise and Corporate Social Responsibility. Evidence from S&P 500 Companies. *International Journal of Law and Management* 55 (3), 161–172.

Tang, Z., Hull, C.E., Rothenber, S. (2012). How Corporate Social Responsibility Engagement Strategy Moderates the CSR – Financial Performance Relationship. *Journal of Management Studies* 49, 1274–1303.

United Nations (1987). *Our Common Future.* Report of the World Commission on Environment and Development. United Nations A/42/427. New York, 4 Aug. 1987. https://digitallibrary.un.org/record/139811?v=pdf

Urbański, S. (2012). Multifactor Explanations of Returns on the Warsaw Stock Exchange in Light of the ICAPM. *Economic Systems* 36 (4), 552–570.

Urbański, S., & Zarzecki, D. (2022). The Fama-French Model for Estimating the Cost of Equity Capital: The Impact of Real Options of Investment Projects. *Economic Systems* 46 (1), 100874.

Vance, S.C. (1975). Are Socially Responsible Corporations Good Investment Risks? *Management Review* 64 (8), 18–24.

Waddock, S.A., & Graves S.B. (1997). The Corporate Social Performance – Financial Performance Link. *Strategic Management Journal* 18 (4), 303–319.

Wang, H., Lu, W., Ye, M., Chau, K.W., & Zhang, X. (2016). The Curvilinear Relationship Between Corporate Social Performance and Corporate Financial Performance: Evidence from the International Construction Industry. *Journal of Cleaner Production* 37, 1313–1322.

Yusoff, H., Mohamad, S.S., & Darus, F. (2013). The Influence of CSR Disclosure Structure on Corporate Financial Performance: Evidence from Stakeholders' Perspective. *Procedia Economics and Finance* 7, 213–220.

Zhou, W. (2022). Is ESG a Novel Pricing Risk Factor for the Chinese Stock Markets during COVID-19? *Proceedings of the 6th International Conference on Economic Management and Green Development (ICEMGD 2022), Part I. 3.)*. 794-802.

4 Methodology

We analyse the monthly stock returns of the principal indices from the American, European, Japanese, and Chinese markets. The Polish capital market is the largest and most developed among Central and Eastern European emerging markets. Thus, we also examine the Polish market, which may present an alternative investment opportunity to highly developed markets (see Table 4.1).[1]

The companies selected for the portfolios are drawn from the benchmark indices and are listed within the following historical periods:

- **Standard & Poor's 500 Index (S&P 500)**: January 1995 to March 2022, covering 311 monthly investment periods.
- **Bloomberg Europe 500 Index (BE 500)**: January 2000 to March 2022, covering 251 monthly investment periods.
- **Tokyo Stock Price Index 500 (TOPIX 500)**: January 2003 to March 2022, covering 215 monthly investment periods.
- **Shanghai Stock Exchange 380 Index (SSE 380)**: January 2002 to March 2022, covering 227 monthly investment periods.
- **Warsaw Stock Exchange WIG Index (WIG)**: January 1995 to March 2022, covering 311 monthly investment periods.[2]

We assume that the fund manager acts rationally, in line with FF1995, and believes that future returns are derived from the past structure of financial results. Consequently, the fund manager is an ICAPM investor, who invests in a portfolio unknown to us. This portfolio is simulated using a portfolio of portfolios consisting of 5, 7, 10, and 15 companies from the examined indices, with maximum FUN values. The fund manager adjusts the portfolio composition in periods

DOI: 10.4324/9781003587330-4

Table 4.1 Number of listed companies and values of capitalisation of tested stock indexes in 2021

No.	*Stock index*	*Number of listed companies*	*Value of capitalisation [USD billion]*
1	*S&P 500*	505	41,696
2	*BE 500*	497	13,321
3	*TOPIX 500*	496	5625
4	*SSE 380*	380	1163
5	*WIG*	430	324

Sources: Bloomberg database and www.gpw.pl.

unknown to us, based on the maximisation of FUN. It is assumed that the simulated portfolio can be modified monthly.

The calculation of FUN requires at least 12 consecutive months of data. Using these 12 months of observations, FUN data are available for the following 4 months, resulting in a minimum delay of 16 months for the adopted investment period. The first hypothetical investment can be made after the company publishes its financial results for the first quarterly period.

Figures A.1, A.2, A.3, A.4, and A.5 (provided in the Appendix) illustrate the changes in cumulative returns of the average portfolio, which consists of portfolios of 15, 10, 7, and 5 companies with the highest FUN2012 and FUN2022 functional values. These figures also depict the cumulative returns of the studied indices across the individual markets.

Table A.1 (provided in the Appendix) presents the average annual effective returns for the average portfolio, which consists of portfolios of 15, 10, 7, and 5 companies with the highest FUN2012 and FUN2022 functional values.

The changes in returns from the examined portfolios indicate that the portfolios formed on the basis of FUN2012 yielded higher returns than those formed on the basis of FUN2022 for the Polish, American, and European markets. In contrast, the trends in the Japanese market were reversed. The returns on the Chinese market were similar for portfolios formed using either FUN2012 or FUN2022. The largest relative increases in returns from the generated portfolios, compared to the corresponding market indices, were observed for the European, Japanese, Polish, and American markets, with increases of approximately 650%, 340%, 300%, and 250%, respectively. The smallest relative increase occurred in the Chinese market, at around 160%.

The higher returns of the portfolios formed on FUN2012 in three of the markets warrant explanation. Investors focusing on FUN2012 assess the financial results of companies, while investors using FUN2022 rely on the ratio of financial results to equity. Financial results are typically published after each reporting period, whereas the ratios must be calculated before investment decisions are made. As financial results, rather than their ratios to equity, are more readily available to a broader group of market participants, we opt to model investor portfolios based on FUN2012.

We calculate FUN values for each company at the start of each monthly period. Portfolios of 5, 7, 10, and 15 companies are formed based on the highest FUN2012 values. The stocks in these portfolios are weighted linearly. Returns for these portfolios are then calculated for each monthly period.

The investments of a hypothetical mutual fund investor are generally oriented towards long-term periods. We assume these periods to be 60 and 96 months (5 and 8 years). Therefore, the analysis of changes in returns for hypothetical mutual fund investments is conducted based on average returns in rolling 96- and 60-month time windows.

Rolling average returns for portfolios formed using FUN and the benchmark index portfolio, with a one-month step, are calculated for each market over the entire examined investment period.

To validate the adopted assumptions, we examine the dynamics of the return differences between the benchmark portfolio and the portfolio formed using FUN. Similarly, we analyse the evolution of the differences between the SR of the FUN-formed portfolio and the benchmark portfolio.

The following test procedures are adopted:

a) Modelling of returns and SRs differences

   We focus on inferring the differences in returns and SRs, measuring the outperformance or underperformance of fundamental portfolios relative to the benchmark index. The temporal dynamics of these differences are tracked using time-series methods. The risk-free rate (RF) is estimated for each market based on U.S. 3-month Treasury bills.

b) Time-series forecasting

We employ both the Holt–Winters double exponential smoothing approach and the SARIMA model to forecast the two types of differences. The following provides a brief description of the Holt-Winters model. Given the empirical data $\{X_t\}_{t=1}^{n}$, standard smoothing is performed recursively, with the level $\{l_t\}$ and trend $\{m_t\}$ for $1 \leq t < n$:

$$l_t = \alpha X_{t-1} + (1-\alpha)(l_{t-1} + m_{t-1}) \tag{33}$$

$$m_t = \beta(l_t - l_{t-1}) + (1-\beta)m_{t-1} \tag{34}$$

$$X_{t+1} = l_t + m_t \tag{35}$$

The smoothing parameters $\propto, \beta \in (0;1]$ are either fixed or optimised with respect to specific criteria, such as minimising mean squared error (Chatfield 1978). Forecasts are then defined by:

$$\hat{X}_{n+h} = l_n + h \cdot m_n, \quad h = 1,2,... \tag{36}$$

The second proposed model is SARIMA$(p,d,q)(P,D,Q)[S]$, where X_t follows the SARIMA $(p,d,q)(P,D,Q)[S]$ model:

$$\Phi_P(B^S)\phi(B)\nabla_s^D\nabla^d x_t = \delta + \Theta_Q(B^S)\theta(B)\omega_t \tag{37}$$

Here:

ω_t is the usual Gaussian white noise process;

$\nabla_s^D = (1-B^S)^D$ is the seasonal difference component;

$\nabla^d = (1-B)^d$ is the ordinary difference component;

$\delta = \mu(1-\phi_1 - \ldots - \phi_p)$ and $\mu = E(\nabla^d x_t)$;

$\Phi_P(B^S) = 1 - \Phi_1 B^S - \Phi_2 B^{2S} - \ldots - \Phi_P B^{PS}$ is the seasonal autoregressive component of order P;

$\phi(B) = 1 - \phi_1 B^1 - \phi_2 B^2 - \ldots - \phi_p B^p$ is the ordinary autoregressive component of order p;

$\Theta_Q(B^S) = 1 - \Phi_1 B^S - \Phi_2 B^{2S} - \ldots - \Phi_Q B^{QS}$ is the seasonal moving average component of order Q;

$\theta(B) = 1 - \theta_1 B^1 - \theta_2 B^2 - \ldots - \theta_q B^q$ is the ordinary moving average component of order q;

p, d, q are ARIMA parameters; P, D, Q are SARIMA parameters;

S is the season lag and B is the backshift operator (Shumway and Stoffer 2011).

Models for two variables are developed. The first variable represents the difference between the average return of portfolios formed using FUN (from 60- and 96-month periods) and the benchmark portfolio. The second variable is the difference between the SRs of the FUN-formed portfolio and the benchmark portfolio. Forecasts are made for a 12-month horizon. To test the statistical validity of Conjectures 1 and 2, a 95% confidence interval is constructed. If the forecasted difference lies within this interval, we conclude that the differences are statistically insignificant, implying the market efficiency hypothesis cannot be rejected. These 12-month forecasts are updated every 12 months, starting with the 61st or 97th monthly observation for each market.

c) Rolling dynamic correlations, using a 36-month window, between FUN portfolio and benchmark index returns

The cross-correlations are based on the intervals of the length h selected from both time series R_t^B and R_t^{FUN}, where R_t^B is the return on the benchmark index and R_t^{FUN} corresponds to the portfolio formed on FUN in period t. Given $\{(R_t^B, R_t^{\text{FUN}})\}_{t=T-h+1}^{T}$ we calculate the Pearson cross-correlation coefficient.

$$\hat{\rho}(T) = \frac{\hat{\gamma}(T)}{\hat{\sigma}^B \hat{\sigma}^{\text{FUN}}} \tag{38}$$

where

$$\hat{\gamma}(T) = \frac{1}{h} \sum_{s=T-h+1}^{T} \left(R_s^B - \bar{R}^B\right)\left(R_s^{FUN} - \bar{R}^{FUN}\right) \tag{39}$$

$$\bar{R}^B = \frac{1}{h} \sum_{s=T-h+1}^{T} R_s^B \tag{40}$$

$$\bar{R}^{\mathrm{FUN}} = \frac{1}{h} \sum_{s=T-h+1}^{T} R_s^{\mathrm{FUN}} \tag{41}$$

$$\hat{\sigma}^B = \sqrt{\frac{1}{h-1} \sum_{s=T-h+1}^{T} \left(R_s^B - \bar{R}^B\right)} \tag{42}$$

$$\hat{\sigma}^{FUN} = \sqrt{\frac{1}{h-1} \sum_{s=T-h+1}^{T} \left(R_s^{FUN} - \bar{R}^{FUN}\right)} \tag{43}$$

The dynamic cross-correlation profiles are obtained by moving T along the data, yielding a sequence $\{\hat{\rho}(T)\}_{T=h}^{n}$.

To validate Conjecture 3, we calculate the average capitalisation values of the FUN portfolios and the 50 largest-cap stocks of the benchmark index. Stocks are weighted by market capitalisation, meaning that large-cap stocks have a dominant effect on the returns of the index. If the FUN portfolios consist of large-cap stocks, the returns of the FUN and benchmark portfolios are expected to be similar.

To evaluate the economic significance of FUN, without relying on changes in risk or the correct pricing of capital, we model the cross-sectional relationship between expected returns and the functional value of FUN. Equation (44) expresses the impact of average FUN values at the end of period $t-1$ ($t=2;n$) on the average returns over periods t ($t=1,n-1$).

$$\bar{r}_i = a_0 + a_1 \overline{\mathrm{FUN}}_i + \varepsilon_i \tag{44}$$

where $i = 1, \ldots, m$.

Table 4.2 presents the dependence of average quintile/decile returns of portfolios formed from the 100 companies with the highest FUN values on the average FUN values of these portfolios.
Cross-sectional regressions reveal a linear, positive relationship between average returns and FUN values.

Table 4.3 presents summary statistics for the tested benchmark indexes, while Table 4.4 provides summary statistics for portfolios formed on the same benchmark indexes.

Table 4.2 Values of the cross-sectional regression coefficients of the dependence of the average returns on the FUN values determined by the classic method of least squares

a_0	$serr(a_0)$	*p-value (%)*	a_1	$serr(a_1)$	*p-value (%)*	R^2 *(%)*
Panel A: *S&P 500*; tested period: 1996–2022; 312 months						
0.009/ 0.009	0.003/ 0.002	0.37/ 0.00	0.003/ 0.003	0.001/ 0.001	1.59/ 0.05	60.59/ 57.71
Panel B: *BE500*; tested period: 2001–2022; 252 months						
0.006/ 0.007	0.003/ 0.002	0.69/ 0.00	0.004/ 0.004	0.001/ 0.001	0.01/ 0.00	82.16/ 79.30
Panel C: *TOPIX 500*; tested period: 2004–2022; 216 months						
0.000/ 0.004	0.003/ 0.004	46.00/ 19.88	0.004/ 0.003	0.001/ 0.002	0.04/ 5.60	78.80/ 24.02
Panel D: *SSE 380*; tested period: 2003–2022; 227 months						
0.004/ 0.004	0.004/ 0.002	17.04/ 3.29	0.006/ 0.005	0.002/ 0.001	0.01/ 0.00	82.80/ 78.12
Panel E: *WIG*; tested period: 1996–2022; 312 months						
0.004/ 0.003	0.004/ 0.005	19.70/ 28.33	0.006/ 0.006	0.002/ 0.002	0.23/ 0.23	72.75/ 50.09

$\overline{r_i} = a_0 + a_1 \overline{\text{FUN}_i} + \varepsilon_i;\ i = 1, \ldots, 5(\text{quintiles})/10(\text{deciles})$

Source: Own calculations.

Notes: The study concerns 100 companies from the tested indexes with the highest FUN values; serr – standard error, $\overline{\text{FUN}_i}$ – average FUN value over time for quintile/decile portfolio i determined at the end of periods $t-1$; $\overline{r_i}$ – average return of quintile/decile portfolio i determined from periods t. The portfolios are linearly weighted.

Table 4.3 Summary statistics for tested indexes

Index	*Mean (min; max) (%)*	*Median (%)*	*Standard deviations (%)*	*t-Statistic*	*Kurtosis*	*Skewness*
Panel A: Monthly returns on tested historical period						
WIG	0.72 (-29.6; 23.7)	0.62	6.68	1.90	2.14	-0.15
S&P 500	0.88 (-16.8; 12.8)	1.34	4.38	3.58	1.10	-0.60
BE 500	0.51 (-21.1; 17.5)	0.77	5.35	1.52	1.41	-0.45
TOPIX 500	0.43 (-14.4; 12.1)	0.60	4.17	1.52	1.08	-0.30
SSE 380	1.48 (-29.2; 37.8)	1.34	9.08	2.38	1.81	0.05
Panel B: Moving average monthly returns on 96 months						
WIG	0.79 (-0.05; 1.76)	0.78	0.47	16.5	-0.91	0.30
S&P 500	0.69 (-0.29; 1.47)	0.65	0.39	26.3	-0.62	-0.09
BE 500	0.57 (0.08; 1.15)	0.59	0.23	31.7	0.07	0.02
TOPIX 500	0.44 (-0.04; 0.86)	0.55	0.26	18.5	-1.58	-0.17
SSE 380	1.41 (0.21; 2.59)	1.28	0.66	24.8	-1.22	0.09

Source: Own calculations.

Notes: Tested periods: *S&P 500*: from May 1996 through March 2022; *BE 500*: from May 2001 through March 2022; *TOPIX 500*: from May 2004 through March 2022; *SSE 380*: from May 2003 through March 2022; *WIG*: from May 1996 through March 2022.

Both tables (4.3 and 4.4) show that averaging returns over 96 months results in greater regularity. For most cases, kurtosis and skewness for averaged data are closer to zero than for raw data. The averaged portfolios exhibit more regularity than the raw portfolios.

Notes

1 The financial data required to calculate FUN are sourced from the Bloomberg Terminal. Data on the investor composition in the analysed markets are provided by the EquityRT service via Notoria Serwis SA and S&P Global

Table 4.4 Summary statistics for portfolio formed on tested indexes

Index	*Mean (min; max) (%)*	*Median (%)*	*Stand. dev. (%)*	*t-Statistic*	*Kurtosis*	*Skewness*
Panel A: Monthly returns on tested historical period						
AvPOR WIG	2.67 (-28.2; 53.2)	1.93	10.39	4.53	2.34	0.52
AvPOR S&P 500	2.04 (-15.9; 28.5)	2.02	6.27	5.75	1.59	0.28
AvPOR BE 500	1.95 (-28.6; 28.6)	2.23	6.88	4.46	2.27	-0.39
AvPOR TOPIX 500	1.30 (-15.4; 15.6)	1.47	5.37	3.54	0.44	0.05
AvPOR SSE 380	2.38 (-27.8; 44.6)	1.62	10.11	3.56	1.99	0.44
Panel B: Moving average monthly returns on 96 months						
AvPOR WIG	2.96 (0.35; 6.22)	2.89	1.60	18.17	-1.19	0.28
AvPOR S&P 500	1.96 (1.15; 2.95)	1.87	0.46	62.35	-0.97	0.39
AvPOR BE 500	1.69 (1.01; 2.52)	1.80	0.37	56.86	-0.94	-0.10
AvPOR TOPIX 500	1.31 (0.85; 1.76)	1.30	0.20	71.46	-0.74	0.20
AvPOR SSE 380	2.28 (1.53; 3.02)	2.27	0.36	73.90	-1.02	0.00

Source: Own calculations.

Notes: *AvPOR TOPIX 500*, *AvPOR BE 500*, *AvPOR S&P 500*, *AvPOR WIG*, and *AvPOR SSE 380* are linearly weighted portfolio consisting of 15, 10, 7, and 5 stock portfolios formed on *TOPIX 500, BE 500, S&P 500, WIG,* and *SSE 380* indexes. Linearly weighted portfolios of 15, 10, 7, and 5 stocks are formed based on the maximisation of the *FUN* of all stocks of tested indexes. Tested periods *AvPOR S&P 500*: from May 1996 through March 2022; *AvPOR BE 500*: from May 2001 through March 2022; *AvPOR TOPIX 500*: from May 2004 through March 2022; *AvPOR SSE 380*: from May 2003 through March 2022; *AvPOR WIG*: from May 1996 through March 2022.

Market Intelligence, Morningstar, Factset Estimates by Xignite, Reuters, local exchanges, and other regional data providers. The EquityRT website (www.equityrt.com) is authored by RasyOnet. The service's data providers include S&P Global Market Intelligence, Morningstar, Factset Estimates by Xignite, Reuters, local exchanges, and other local sources.

2 Different historical periods are used due to the availability of data in the Bloomberg database.

References

Chatfield, C. (1978). The Holt-Winters Forecasting Procedure. *Applied Statistics* 27 (3), 264–279.

Fama, E.F., & French, K.R. (1995). Size and Book-to-Market Factors in Earnings and Returns. *Journal of Finance* 50 (1), 131–155.

Shumway, R.H., & Stoffer, D.S. (2011). *Time Series Analysis and Its Applications: With R Examples*. 3rd ed. New York: Springer.

5 Results

In this section, we analyse changes in the averaged rolling returns and rolling SRs of the examined markets. For the reader's convenience, we note that each data point in the figures below represents the start of a 96-month or 60-month investment period.

5.1 U.S. market

Figure 5.1 displays the following: (a) rolling 96-month average returns, (b) rolling correlations between the 96-month returns of the formed portfolio and the S&P 500 index, (c) rolling SRs for 96-month investments in the S&P 500 average portfolio (formed from portfolios of 5, 7, 10, and 15 companies with the highest FUN values), and the S&P 500 index, and (d) rolling correlations between the SRs of the formed portfolios and the S&P 500 index. The correlations are calculated using 36-month windows.
The curves representing the time series of returns and SRs illustrate the changes in the formed portfolios and the index over time.

The highest average returns for 96-month investments in the portfolios of 5, 7, 10, and 15 companies (with the highest FUN values) between 1996 and 2022 are 45.9%, 43.3%, 39.2%, and 38.7% per annum, respectively. The lowest average returns for the same portfolios during the same period are 14.2%, 15.0%, 13.0%, and 15.5% per annum, respectively.

The maximum and minimum average returns for 96-month investments in the average portfolio (comprising the 5, 7, 10, and 15 company portfolios) from 1996 to 2022 are 41.8% and 14.4% per annum, respectively. The maximum and minimum average returns for

DOI: 10.4324/9781003587330-5

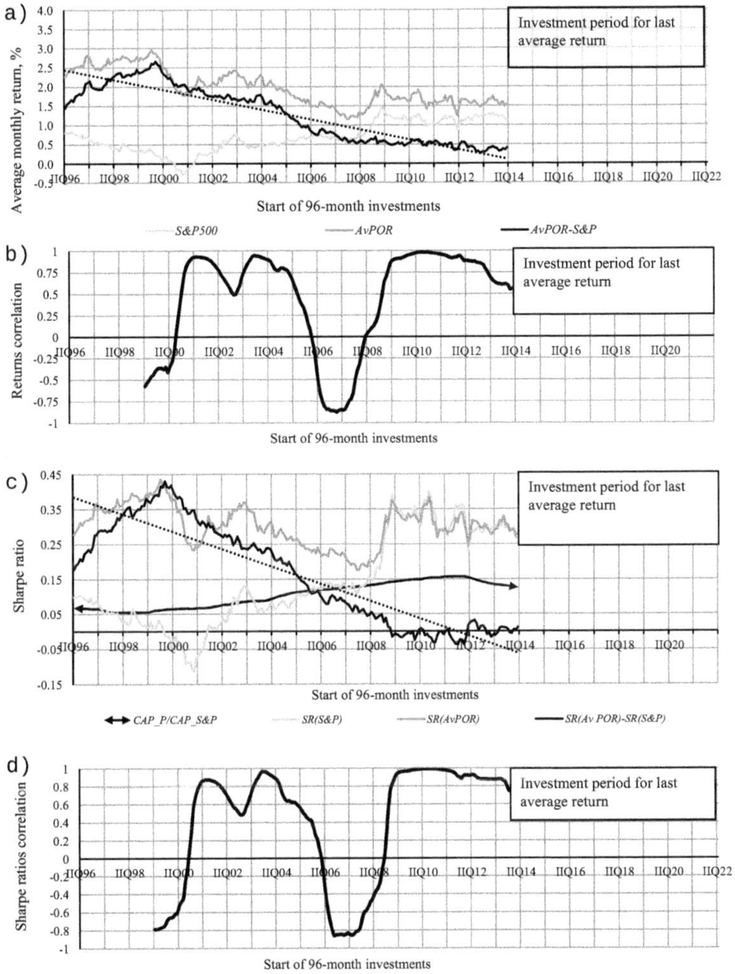

Figure 5.1 Rolling a) 96-month average returns, b) correlations between 96-month average returns of formed portfolio and the *S&P 500* index, c) SR on 96 months: of *S&P 500* formed portfolio and *S&P 500* index, d) correlations between the SR of *S&P 500* formed portfolio and *S&P 500* index.

Notes: *AvPOR* is a linearly weighted portfolio consisting of 15, 10, 7, and 5 stock portfolios formed on *S&P 500* index. Each point of the chart represents the examined portfolio characteristics [average return, correlation between *AvPOR* and *S&P 500*

Figure 5.1 (Continued)

average returns, SR, correlation between SR of *AvPOR* and SR of *S&P 500* index, and ratio of 15 companies portfolio capitalisation (*CAP_P*) to the capitalisation of 50 companies with the maximum capitalisation of the index (*CAP_S&P*)] at the beginning of the 96-month investment period. SR of *AvPOR* is computed as the ratio of the average excess return on *AvPOR* over the average risk-free rate (*AvPOR-RF*) to the standard deviation of the excess return s(*AvPOR-RF*). *RF* is estimated based on U.S. 3-Month Treasury bills. SR of *S&P 500* is computed as the ratio of the average excess return on *S&P 500* over the average risk-free rate (*S&P 500-RF*) to the standard deviation of the excess return s(*S&P 500-RF*). Stock portfolios are formed based on the maximisation of the *FUN* of all stocks of *S&P 500*. The dotted line in Figure a) shows the trend line of changes in the differences between the average return on *AvPOR* and the average return on the *S&P 500* index. The dotted line in Figure c) shows the trend line of changes in the differences between the *SR* of *AvPOR* (*SR(AvPOR)*) and the SR of the *S&P 500* index (*SR(S&P)*). The analysed historical period from May 1996 through March 2022, 311 months.

Source: Own research.

the S&P 500 index during the same period are 19.2% and -3.4% per annum, respectively.

A careful examination of the figures reveals substantial differences between the returns of the formed portfolios and the index from 1996 to 2006. These differences have steadily decreased since 2007, particularly evident in the SR. The trend line difference between the portfolios and the index has fallen from 2.5% to approximately 0% for average returns and from 0.4% to nearly 0% for SRs (see Figures 5.1a and 5.1c).

The largest changes in the correlation coefficients of returns between the formed portfolios and the S&P 500 index occurred between 2005 and 2009. The correlation decreased monotonically from 0.8 in 2005 to -0.9 in 2007, before rising steadily to over 0.9 by 2009. From 2010 onwards, the correlation approached values close to 1. Similar trends are observed in the correlation coefficients of the SRs of the formed portfolios and the S&P 500 index throughout the 1996–2022 period (see Figures 5.1b and 5.1d).

Changes in the relative market capitalisation of the 15-company formed portfolio compared to the 50 largest companies in the S&P 500 index indicate an increase in the portfolio's relative capitalisation starting in 2004, reaching a peak of 15%. A slight decrease (around 2%) is observed post-2012 (see Figure 5.1c). This shift may partly explain the gradual reduction in the differences between the returns of the formed portfolios and the index after 2007.

Figure 5.2 presents the following: (a) rolling 60-month average returns, (b) rolling correlations between the 60-month returns of the formed portfolios and the S&P 500 index, (c) rolling SRs for 60-month investments in the S&P 500 average portfolio (formed from portfolios of 5, 7, 10, and 15 companies with the highest FUN values), and the S&P 500 index, and (d) rolling correlations between the SRs of the formed portfolios and the S&P 500 index. The correlations are calculated using 36-month windows.

The maximum average returns on 60-month investments in portfolios consisting of 5, 7, 10, and 15 companies (with the highest FUN values) during the period 1996–2022 are as follows: 59.8%, 56.2%, 48.9%, and 46.8% annually. Conversely, the minimum average returns on 60-month investments in the same portfolios are 8.9%, 9.5%, 7.9%, and 9.5%, respectively, over the same period.

The maximum and minimum average returns on 60-month investments in the average portfolio (a composite of the portfolios of 5, 7, 10, and 15 companies) from 1996 to 2022 are 52.9% and 9.0% annually, respectively. For the S&P 500 index, the maximum and minimum average returns on 60-month investments over the same period are 24.2% and -5.7% annually, respectively.

A careful examination of these figures reveals significant differences between the return values of the formed portfolios and the index during the years 1996–2006. Notably, these differences have decreased since 2007, particularly in the SR. The trend line of differences shows a decline from 2.5% to approximately 0% for average returns, and from 0.4% to nearly 0% for SRs (see Figures 5.2a and 5.2c). These trends are similar to those observed for 96-month investments.

The most significant changes in the correlation coefficients between the returns of the formed portfolios and the S&P 500 index occurred between 2005 and 2009. The correlation decreased monotonically from 0.98 in 2005 to -0.5 in 2007, before increasing again to over 0.98 by 2009. From 2010 onwards, the correlation remained between 0.75 and 0.99. Similar changes in the correlation of SRs for the formed portfolios and the S&P 500 index are evident over the entire 1996–2022 period (see Figures 5.2b and 5.2d).

Changes in the ratio of the capitalisation of the formed portfolio of 15 companies to the capitalisation of the 50 largest companies in the S&P 500 index show that the relative capitalisation of the portfolio began to rise in 2004, peaking at 15%. A slight decrease occurred after 2015 (see Figure 5.2c). This shift may help explain the delayed reduction in the differences between the returns of the formed portfolios

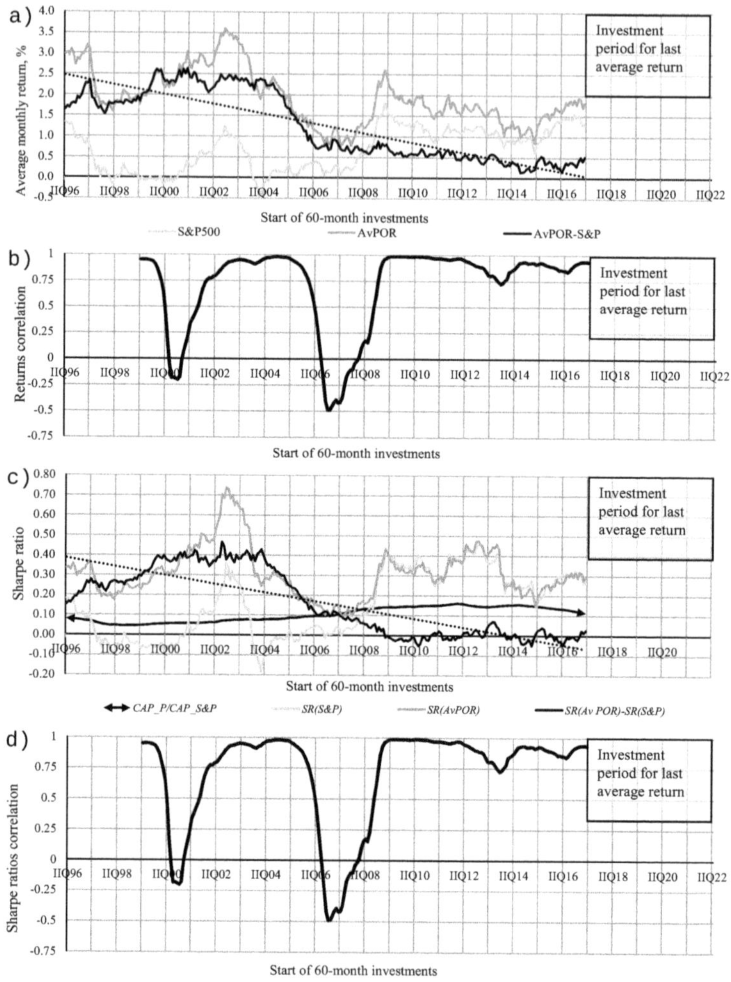

Figure 5.2 Rolling a) 60-month average returns, b) correlations between 60-month average returns of formed portfolio and the *S&P 500* index, c) SR on 60 months: of *S&P 500* formed portfolio and *S&P 500* index, d) correlations between the SR of *S&P 500* formed portfolio and *S&P 500* index.

Notes: *AvPOR* is a linearly weighted portfolio consisting of 15, 10, 7, and 5 stock portfolios formed on *S&P 500* index. Each point of the chart represents the examined portfolio characteristics [average return, correlation between *AvPOR* and *S&P 500*

Figure 5.2 (Continued)

average returns, SR, correlation between SR of *AvPOR* and SR of *S&P 500* index, and ratio of 15 companies portfolio capitalisation (*CAP_P*) to the capitalisation of 50 companies with the maximum capitalisation of the index (*CAP_S&P*)] at the beginning of the 60-month investment period. SR of *AvPOR* is computed as the ratio of the average excess return on *AvPOR* over the average risk-free rate (*AvPOR-RF*) to the standard deviation of the excess return s(*AvPOR-RF*). *RF* is estimated based on U.S. 3-Month Treasury bills. SR of *S&P 500* is computed as the ratio of the average excess return on *S&P 500* over the average risk-free rate (*S&P 500-RF*) to the standard deviation of the excess return s(*S&P 500-RF*). Stock portfolios are formed based on the maximisation of the *FUN* of all stocks of *S&P 500*. The dotted line in Figure a) shows the trend line of changes in the differences between the average return on *AvPOR* and the average return on the *S&P 500* index. The dotted line in Figure c) shows the trend line of changes in the differences between the SR of *AvPOR* (*SR(AvPOR)*) and the SR of the *S&P 500* index (*SR(S&P)*). The analysed historical period from May 1996 through March 2022, 311 months.

Source: Own research.

and the index after 2007. These trends are comparable to those for 96-month investments.

To better assess the dynamics of the time series for the formed portfolios and the S&P 500 index, we employ additional statistical methods. Specifically, we analyse the time series of the differences in returns (AvPOR-S&P) and SRs (SR(AvPOR)-SR(S&P)) for the formed portfolios and the index.

Figure 5.3 presents the SARIMA model used to forecast the rolling differences between the 96-month average returns and SRs for the formed portfolios and the S&P 500 index.

The order of the SARIMA model was selected based on the AIC criterion (for more on AIC, see Shumway and Stoffer 2011). Table 5.1 presents the parameter estimates for this model.

The available data allow for the calculation of forecasts and confidence intervals for return and SR differences since Q2 2004. The SARIMA model indicates that the forecasted confidence intervals for SR differences over 96-month periods (denoted SRs96) begin to include zero from Q2 2006 onwards (see Figure 5.3b). This suggests that there is no statistically significant difference between the SR of the FUN portfolio and the S&P 500 benchmark portfolio. As such, we propose that Conjecture 2 be rejected. Notably, the most recent forecast indicates that the difference between the SRs96 of the formed portfolios and the S&P 500 portfolio is tending towards zero.

The market's shift towards efficiency is also evident in the return differences. The forecasted confidence intervals for return differences

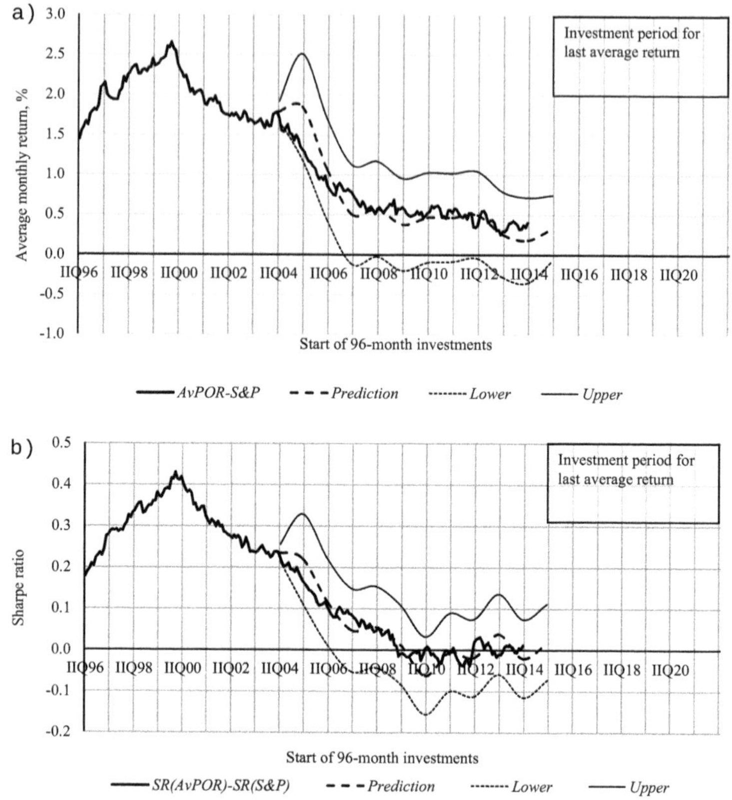

Figure 5.3 SARIMA and prediction of rolling differences between a) the 96-month average returns, b) SR on 96 months, corresponding to the formed portfolios and the values of *S&P 500* index.

Notes: Each point of the chart presents the examined portfolio characteristics (average return and SR) at the beginning of the 96-month investment period. SR is computed as the ratio of the average excess return from the examined portfolio over the average risk-free rate (*Rp-RF*) to the standard deviation of the excess return s(*Rp-RF*). *RF* is estimated based on U.S. 3-Month Treasury bills. *AvPOR* is a linearly weighted portfolio consisting of 15, 10, 7, and 5 stock portfolios formed on *S&P 500* index. Stock portfolios are formed based on the maximisation of the *FUN* of all stocks of *S&P 500*. The dashed thin top and bottom lines are the upper and lower bounds of the forecast confidence intervals. The dashed thick line represents the forecast values of the rolling return difference – in Figure a), and SR difference – in Figure b). The analysed historical period from May 1996 through March 2022, 311 months.

Source: Own research using R-Studio ver. 4.2.3.

Table 5.1 SARIMA model parameters, base period, and prediction period for rolling differences between average returns and SR on 96 months, corresponding to the formed portfolios and the values of S&P 500 index

SARIMA parameters for season S=12 Months						*Base period*	*Prediction period*	*SARIMA coefficients*				
p	*d*	*q*	*P*	*D*	*Q*			*const*	φ_1	θ_1	Φ_1	Φ_2
Average returns differences												
0	2	1				05.96-04.04	05.04-04.05			-0.9166 ***		
0	2	1				05.96-04.05	05.05-04.06			-0.9299 ***		
0	2	1				05.96-04.06	05.06-04.07			-0.9275 ***		
0	2	1				05.96-04.07	05.07-04.08			-0.9326 ***		
0	2	1				05.96-04.08	05.08-04.09			-0.9361 ***		
0	2	1	2	0	0	05.96-04.09	05.09-04.10			-0.9434 ***	-0.0077	-0.0396
1	2	1				05.96-04.10	05.10-04.11		-0.0243	-0.9372 ***		
1	2	1				05.96-04.11	05.11-04.12		-0.0199	-0.9399 ***		
1	2	1				05.96-04.12	05.12-04.13		-0.0257	-0.9434 ***		
1	2	1				05.96-04.13	05.13-04.14		-0.0034	-0.9491 ***		
0	1	0	2	0	0	05.96-04.14	05.14-04.15	-0.005			-0.0409	0.0096

(*Continued*)

Table 5.1 (Continued)

SARIMA parameters for season S=12 Months						*Base period*	*Prediction period*	*SARIMA coefficients*				
p	*d*	*q*	*P*	*D*	*Q*			*const*	φ_1	θ_1	Φ_1	Φ_2
SR differences												
0	2	1				05.96-04.04	05.04-04.05			-0.9160 ***		
0	2	1				05.96-04.05	05.05-04.06			-0.9209 ***		
0	2	1				05.96-04.06	05.06-04.07			-0.9218 ***		
0	2	1				05.96-04.07	05.07-04.08			-0.9235 ***		
0	2	1				05.96-04.08	05.08-04.09			-0.9279 ***		
0	2	1	1	0	0	05.96-04.09	05.09-04.10			-0.9376 ***	0.0950	
0	2	1	1	0	0	05.96-04.10	05.10-04.11			-0.9376 ***	0.0603	
0	2	1	1	0	0	05.96-04.11	05.11-04.12			-0.9398 ***	0.0409	
0	2	1	1	0	0	05.96-04.12	05.12-04.13			-0.9385 ***	0.0333	
0	2	1	1	0	0	05.96-04.13	05.13-04.14			-0.9447 ***	0.0339	
0	2	1	1	0	0	05.96-04.14	05.14-04.15			-0.9456 ***	0.0443	

Source: Own calculations using R-Studio ver. 4.2.3.

Notes: Significance of coefficients: ***p-value <0.01, **p-value<0.05, *p-value<0.1. The parameters p,d,q correspond to ARIMA model while P, D, Q are related to its seasonal component.

begin to include zero from Q4 2006 (see Figure 5.3a), supporting the rejection of Conjecture 1.

Figure 5.4 illustrates the application of the Holt–Winters method to predict the rolling differences between the 96-month average returns and SRs of the formed portfolios and the S&P 500 index.

Table 5.2 presents the key parameters of the Holt–Winters method.

The Holt–Winters model shows that the confidence intervals for forecasted SR differences (SRs96) consistently include zero from Q2 2006 onwards (see Figure 5.4b). This provides further grounds for rejecting Conjecture 2. As with the SARIMA model, the most recent forecast suggests that the differences between the SRs96 of the formed portfolios and the S&P 500 portfolio are approaching zero.

Similarly, the market's move towards efficiency is reflected in the return differences. The confidence intervals for forecasted return differences approach zero from Q2 2006 onwards (see Figure 5.4a), confirming the rejection of Conjecture 1. These findings align with the results obtained using the SARIMA model.

Figure 5.5 presents the SARIMA model applied to forecast the rolling differences between the 60-month average returns and SRs for the formed portfolios and the S&P 500 index.

In Table A.2 (provided in the Appendix), we present the key parameters of the applied SARIMA model. The available data are used to calculate confidence intervals for forecasts of differences in returns and SRs as of Q2 2001. The SARIMA model indicates that the confidence interval of the forecasted differences in SRs over 60-month periods (hereafter referred to as SRs60) includes zero from Q2 2006 onwards (see Figure 5.5b). This suggests that there is no statistically significant difference between the SR of the FUN portfolio and the S&P 500 benchmark portfolio, providing grounds to reject Conjecture 2. Notably, the latest forecast indicates that the difference between the SRs60 of the formed portfolios and the S&P 500 portfolio tends towards zero, a trend similar to that observed for 96-month investments.

The market's movement towards efficiency is further supported by the forecasted return differences. The confidence interval of the return difference forecasts includes zero from Q4 2006 (see Figure 5.5a), with changes comparable to those for 96-month investments. This supports the rejection of Conjecture 1.

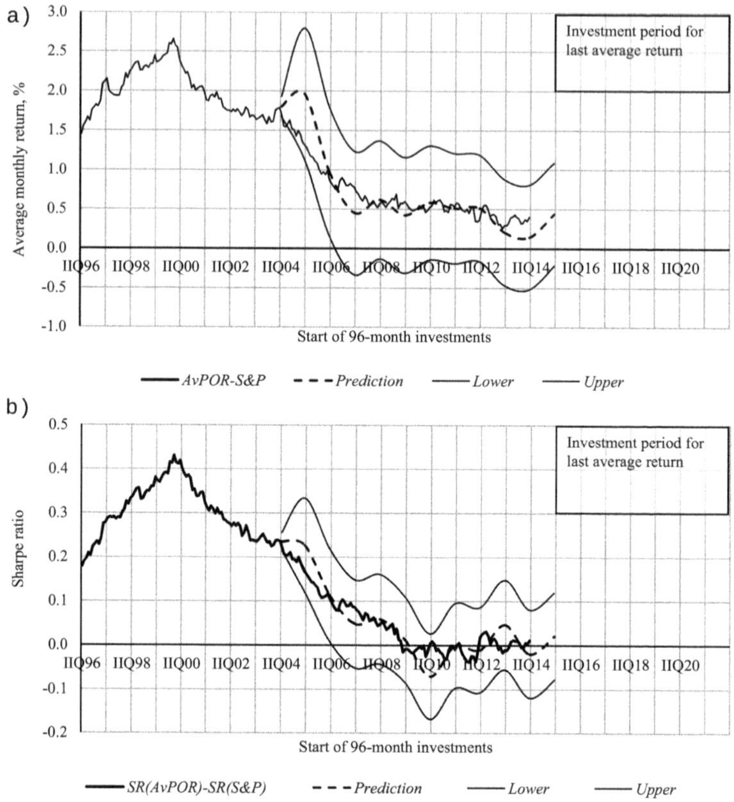

Figure 5.4 Holt–Winters method to predict rolling differences between a) the 96-month average returns, b) SR on 96 months, corresponding to the formed portfolios and the values of *S&P 500* index.

Notes: Each point of the chart presents the examined portfolio characteristics (average return and SR) at the beginning of the 96-month investment period. SR is computed as the ratio of the average excess return from the examined portfolio over the average risk-free rate (*Rp-RF*) to the standard deviation of the excess return s(*Rp-RF*). *RF* is estimated based on U.S. 3-Month Treasury bills. *AvPOR* is a linearly weighted portfolio consisting of 15, 10, 7, and 5 stock portfolios formed on *S&P 500* index. Stock portfolios are formed based on the maximisation of the *FUN* of all stocks of *S&P 500*. The dashed thin top and bottom lines are the upper and lower bounds of the forecast confidence intervals. The dashed thick line represents the forecast values of the rolling return difference – in Figure a), and SR difference – in Figure b). The analysed historical period from May 1996 through March 2022, 311 months.

Source: Own research using ITSM ver. 7.1.

Table 5.2 Holt–Winters method parameters, base period, and prediction period for rolling differences between average returns and SR on 96 months, corresponding to the formed portfolios and the values of S&P 500 index

Holt–Winters parameters		*Base period*	*Prediction period*
α	β		
Average returns differences			
0.97	0.15	05.1996-04.2004	05.2004-04.2005
1	0.13	05.1996-04.2005	05.2005-04.2006
0.99	0.13	05.1996-04.2006	05.2006-04.2007
1	0.12	05.1996-04.2007	05.2007-04.2008
1	0.12	05.1996-04.2008	05.2008-04.2009
0.98	0.12	05.1996-04.2009	05.2009-04.2010
0.97	0.12	05.1996-04.2010	05.2010-04.2011
0.98	0.11	05.1996-04.2011	05.2011-04.2012
0.97	0.11	05.1996-04.2012	05.2012-04.2013
0.99	0.1	05.1996-04.2013	05.2013-04.2014
1	0.1	05.1996-04.2014	05.2014-04.2015
SR differences			
0.86	0.12	05.1996-04.2004	05.2004-04.2005
0.89	0.11	05.1996-04.2005	05.2005-04.2006
0.91	0.1	05.1996-04.2006	05.2006-04.2007
0.94	0.1	05.1996-04.2007	05.2007-04.2008
0.94	0.09	05.1996-04.2008	05.2008-04.2009
0.88	0.1	05.1996-04.2009	05.2009-04.2010
0.87	0.1	05.1996-04.2010	05.2010-04.2011
0.91	0.09	05.1996-04.2011	05.2011-04.2012
0.97	0.08	05.1996-04.2012	05.2012-04.2013
0.99	0.07	05.1996-04.2013	05.2013-04.2014
1	0.07	05.1996-04.2014	05.2014-04.2015

Source: Own calculations using ITSM ver. 7.1.

Notes: α, β – for more details see formula (3) and Chatfield (1978).

Figure 5.6 illustrates the application of the Holt–Winters method to predict rolling differences between the 60-month average returns and SRs of the formed portfolios relative to the S&P 500 index values.

In Table A.3 (provided in the Appendix), we present the key parameters of the Holt–Winters method. This method shows that the confidence interval of the forecasted SRs60 differences continuously includes zero from Q3 2006 onwards (see Figure 5.6b). As such, we

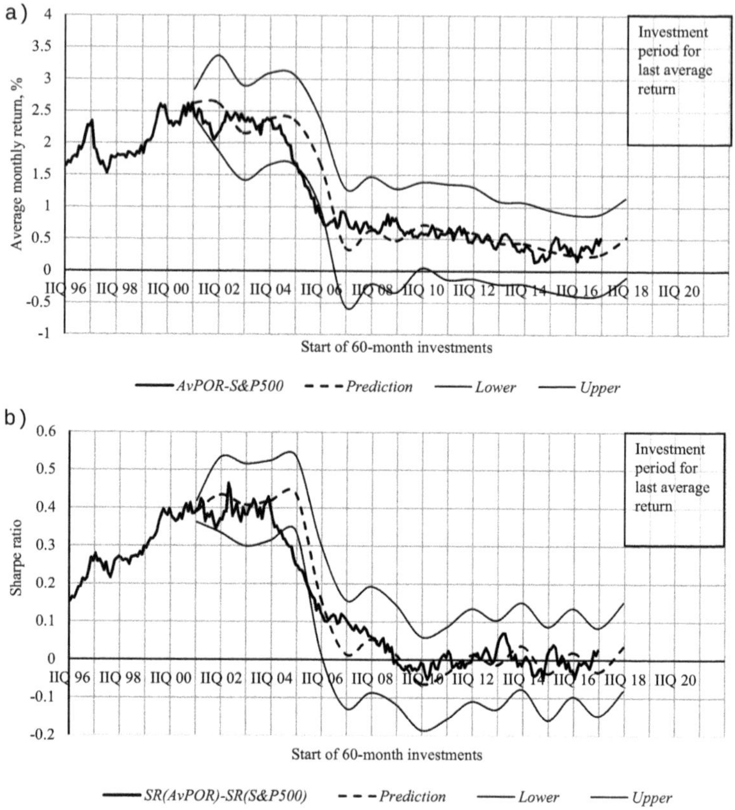

Figure 5.5 SARIMA and prediction of rolling differences between a) the 60-month average returns, b) SR on 60 months, corresponding to the formed portfolios and the values of *S&P 500* index.

Notes: Each point of the chart presents the examined portfolio characteristics (average return and SR) at the beginning of the 60-month investment period. SR is computed as the ratio of the average excess return from the examined portfolio over the average risk-free rate (*Rp-RF*) to the standard deviation of the excess return s(*Rp-RF*). *RF* is estimated based on U.S. 3-Month Treasury bills. *AvPOR* is a linearly weighted portfolio consisting of 15, 10, 7, and 5 stock portfolios formed on *S&P 500* index. Stock portfolios are formed based on the maximisation of the *FUN* of all stock of *S&P 500*. The dashed thin top and bottom lines are the upper and lower bounds of the forecast confidence intervals. The dashed thick line represents the forecast values of rolling return difference – in Figure a), and SR difference – in Figure b). The analysed historical period from May 1996 through March 2022, 311 months.

Source: Own research using R-Studio ver. 4.2.3.

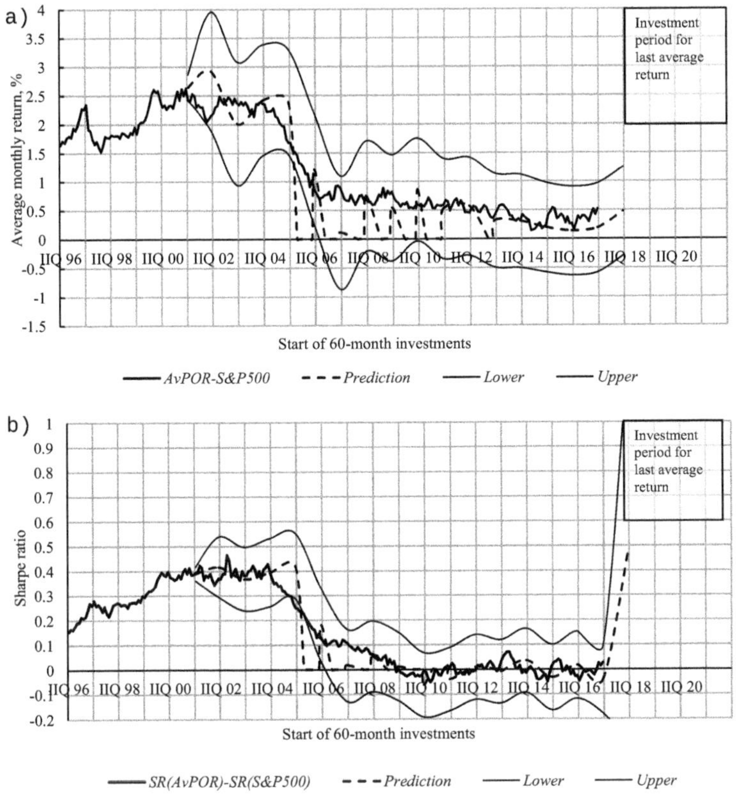

Figure 5.6 Holt–Winters method to predict rolling differences between a) the 60-month average returns, b) SR on 60 months, corresponding to the formed portfolios and the values of *S&P 500* index.

Notes: Each point of the chart presents the examined portfolio characteristics (average return and SR) at the beginning of the 60-month investment period. SR is computed as the ratio of the average excess return from the examined portfolio over the average risk-free rate (*Rp-RF*) to the standard deviation of the excess return s(*Rp-RF*). *RF* is estimated based on U.S. 3-Month Treasury bills. *AvPOR* is a linearly weighted portfolio consisting of 15, 10, 7, and 5 stock portfolios formed on *S&P 500* index. Stock portfolios are formed based on the maximisation of the *FUN* of all stocks of *S&P 500*. The dashed thin top and bottom lines are the upper and lower bounds of the forecast confidence intervals. The dashed thick line represents the forecast values of the rolling return difference – in Figure a), and SR difference – in Figure b). The analysed historical period from May 1996 through March 2022, 311 months.

Source: Own research using ITSM ver. 7.1.

can conclude that, for these periods, there is sufficient evidence to reject Conjecture 2. The latest forecast similarly suggests that the differences between the SRs60 of the formed portfolios and the S&P 500 portfolio tend towards zero, aligning with trends observed for 96-month investments. These results are consistent with those from the SARIMA model.

Likewise, the market's shift towards efficiency is reflected in the return differences. The confidence interval for the forecasted return differences approaches zero from Q2 2006 (see Figure 5.6a), with patterns similar to those for 96-month investments. This further supports the rejection of Conjecture 1. These findings align with the results obtained using the SARIMA model.

5.2 European market

Figure 5.7 presents the rolling 96-month average returns (a), rolling correlations between the 96-month returns of the formed portfolio and the BE 500 index (b), rolling SRs for 96-month periods of the BE 500 average portfolio (formed using the 5, 7, 10, and 15 companies with the highest FUN values) and the BE 500 index (c), and rolling correlations between the SRs of the BE 500 portfolios and the BE 500 index (d). The correlations are calculated using 36-month windows. The curves representing the time series of returns and SRs illustrate the temporal variations of the formed portfolios and the index.

The maximum average returns for 96-month investments in portfolios of 5, 7, 10, and 15 companies (with the highest FUN values) between 2001 and 2022 are 35.2%, 34.5%, 36.0%, and 33.6%, respectively (annualised). Conversely, the minimum average returns for these portfolios during the same period are 12.2%, 12.7%, 14.6%, and 11.6% (annualised).

The maximum and minimum average returns for 96-month investments in the average portfolio (comprising the portfolios of 5, 7, 10, and 15 companies) over the same period are 34.8% and 12.8% (annualised).

For the BE 500 index, the maximum and minimum average returns for 96-month investments between 2001 and 2022 are 14.7% and 0.9%, respectively (annualised).

A careful examination of the figures reveals significant differences between the returns of the formed portfolios and the index portfolio. The trend line for these return differences remains relatively constant,

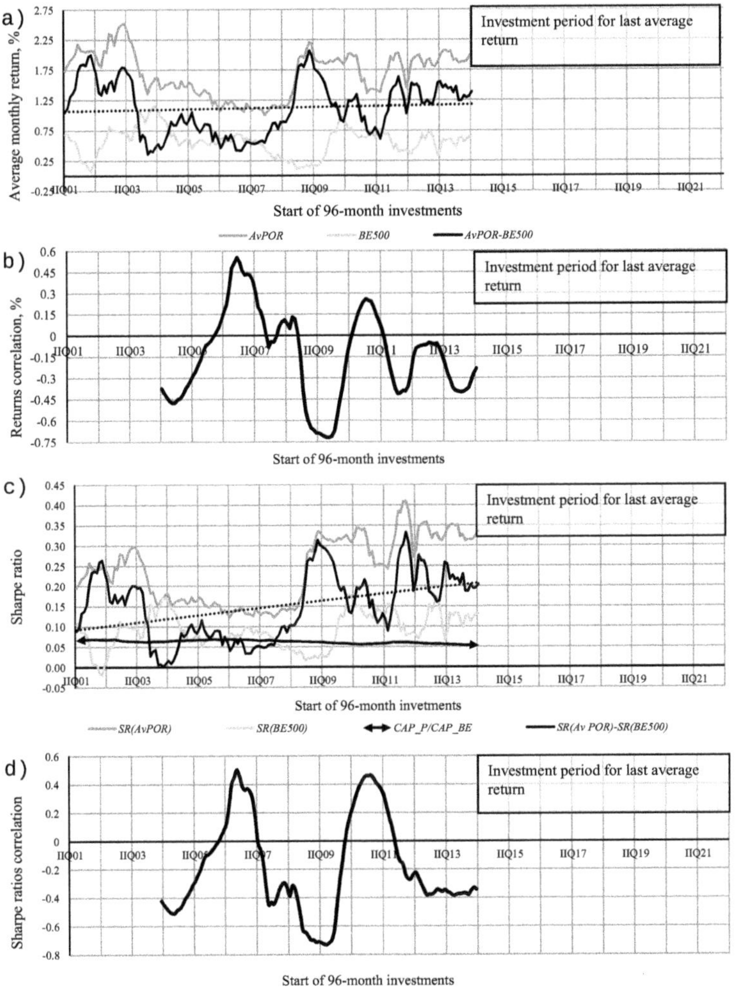

Figure 5.7 Rolling a) 96-month average returns, b) correlations between 96-month average returns of formed portfolio and the *BE 500* index, c) SR on 96 months: of *BE 500* formed portfolio and *BE 500* index, d) correlations between SR of *BE 500* formed portfolio and *BE 500* index.

Notes: *AvPOR* is a linearly weighted portfolio consisting of 15, 10, 7, and 5 stock portfolios formed on *BE 500* index. Each point of the chart represents the examined portfolio characteristics [average return, correlations between *AvPOR* and *BE 500*

Figure 5.7 (Continued)

average returns, SR, correlations between SR of *AvPOR* and SR of *BE 500* index, and the ratio of 15 companies portfolio capitalisation (*CAP_P*) to the capitalisation of 50 companies with the maximum capitalisation of the index (*CAP_BE*)] at the beginning of the 96-month investment period. SR of *AvPOR* is computed as the ratio of the average excess return on *AvPOR* over the average risk-free rate (*AvPOR-RF*) to the standard deviation of the excess return s(*AvPOR-RF*). *RF* is estimated based on U.S. 3-Month Treasury bills. SR of *BE 500* is computed as the ratio of the average excess return on *BE 500* over the average risk-free rate (*BE 500-RF*) to the standard deviation of the excess return s(*BE 500-RF*). Stock portfolios are formed based on the maximisation of the *FUN* of all stocks of *BE 500*. The dotted line in Figure a) shows the trend line of changes in the differences between the average return on *AvPOR* and the average return on the *BE 500* index. The dotted line in Figure c) shows the trend line of changes in the differences between the SR of *AvPOR* (*SR(AvPOR)*) and the SR of the *BE 500* index (*SR(BE 500)*). The analysed historical period from May 2001 through March 2022, 251 months.

Source: Own research.

approximately 1% per month. For the SR, the trend line shows an increase from 0.1 to 0.2 (see Figures 5.7a and 5.7c).

Notable periodic changes in the correlation coefficient between the returns of the formed portfolios and the BE 500 index are evident from 2005 onwards. The correlation decreased from about 0.6 in 2007 to -0.6 in 2009, a trend that contrasts with the broader U.S. market. From 2011 onwards, the correlation fluctuated between 0.2 and -0.4. Similarly, significant changes in the correlation of the SRs between the formed portfolios and the BE 500 index are observed throughout the period 2001–2022 (see Figures 5.7b and 5.7d).

In contrast to the U.S. market, the relative capitalisation of the FUN-formed portfolio remains relatively constant at around 6% (see Figure 5.7c). This suggests that the 15 companies with the highest FUN values have smaller capitalisations in comparison to the BE 500 index, relative to the broader U.S. market.

To further assess the dynamics of the time series for the formed portfolios and the BE 500 index, we employ additional statistical methods. Specifically, we analyse the time series of the differences in returns (AvPOR - BE 500) and SRs (SR(AvPOR) - SR(BE 500)) between the formed portfolios and the index.

Figure 5.8 presents the rolling 60-month average returns (a), rolling correlations between the 60-month returns of the formed portfolios and the BE 500 index (b), rolling SRs for 60-month periods of the BE 500 average portfolio (formed using the 5, 7, 10, and 15 companies with the highest FUN values) and the BE 500 index (c), and rolling correlations between the SRs of the BE 500 portfolios and the BE 500 index (d). The correlations are calculated using 36-month windows. The time series of returns and SRs demonstrate the evolving trends of the formed portfolios and the index.

The maximum average returns for 60-month investments in portfolios of 5, 7, 10, and 15 companies (with the highest FUN values) between 2001 and 2022 are 60.9%, 57.6%, 56.4%, and 56.8%, respectively (annualised). The minimum average returns for these portfolios during the same period are -2.8%, 0.6%, 3.0%, and 1.0% (annualised).

The maximum and minimum average returns for 60-month investments in the average portfolio (comprising the portfolios of 5, 7, 10, and 15 companies) are 57.9% and 1.9%, respectively (annualised).

For the BE 500 index, the maximum and minimum average returns for 60-month investments between 2001 and 2022 are 27.3% and -5.2%, respectively (annualised).

As with the 96-month data, the analysis reveals large differences between the returns of the formed portfolios and the index. The characteristic trend line for return differences remains approximately constant at 1% per month, while the SR trend line increases from 0.1 to 0.2 (see Figures 5.8a and 5.8c).

The correlation coefficient of the returns of the formed portfolios and the BE 500 index also exhibit periodic changes, particularly from 2005 onwards. The correlation decreased from around 0.5 in 2007 to -0.6 in 2009, contrasting with trends in the U.S. market. From 2011 onwards, the correlation fluctuated between 0.3 and -0.5. Similarly, the largest changes in the correlation of the SRs between the formed portfolios and the BE 500 index are observed throughout the 2001–2022 period (see Figures 5.8b and 5.8d).

Again, in contrast to the U.S. market, the relative capitalisation of the FUN-formed portfolio remains roughly constant at about 6% (see Figure 5.8c). This suggests that the 15 companies with the highest FUN values have relatively smaller capitalisations compared to the BE 500 index.

To unambiguously evaluate the dynamics of the time series related to the formed portfolios and the BE 500 index, we employ additional statistical methods. This involves analysing the time series of the differences in returns (AvPOR - BE 500) and SRs (SR(AvPOR) - SR(BE 500)) between the formed portfolios and the index.

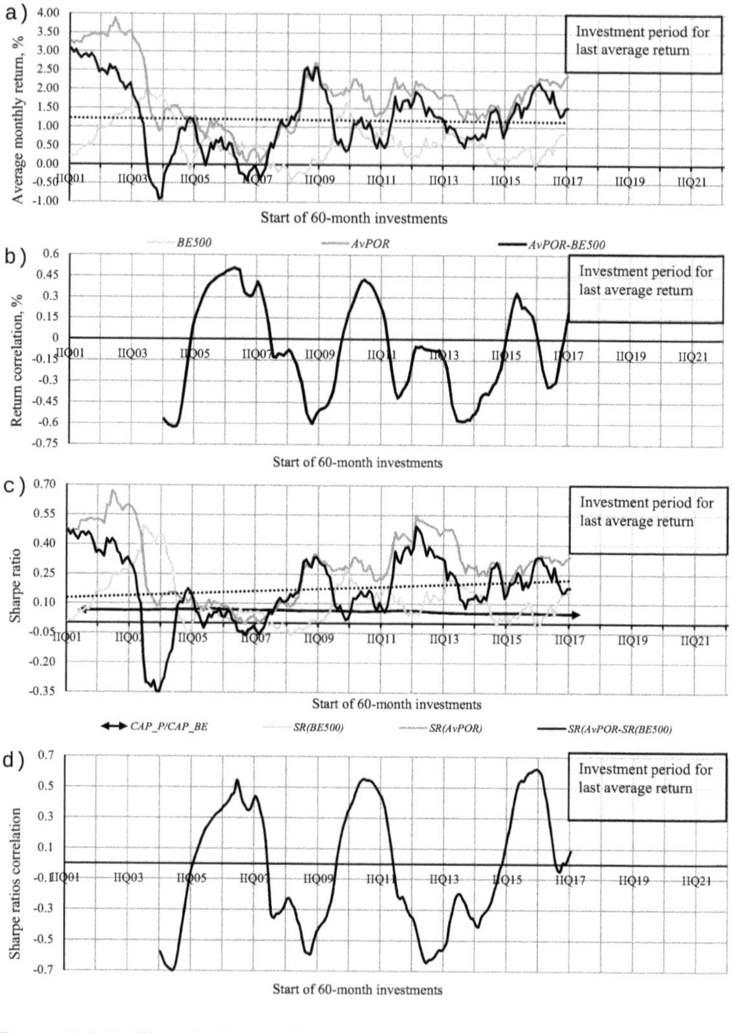

Figure 5.8 Rolling a) 60-month average returns, b) correlations between 60-month average returns of formed portfolio and the *BE 500* index, c) *SR* on 60 months: of *BE 500* formed portfolio and *BE 500* index, d) correlations between the *SR* of *BE 500* formed portfolio and *BE 500* index.

Notes: *AvPOR* is a linearly weighted portfolio consisting of 15, 10, 7, and 5 stock portfolios formed on *BE 500* index. Each point of the chart represents the examined portfolio characteristics [average return, correlations between *AvPOR* and *BE 500* average

Figure 5.8 (Continued)

returns, *SR*, correlations between *SR* of *AvPOR* and *SR* of *BE 500* index, and ratio of 15 companies portfolio capitalisation (*CAP_P*) to the capitalisation of 50 companies with the maximum capitalisation of the index (*CAP_BE*)] at the beginning of the 60-month investment period. *SR* of *AvPOR* is computed as the ratio of the average excess return on *AvPOR* over the average risk-free rate (*AvPOR-RF*) to the standard deviation of the excess return s(*AvPOR-RF*). *RF* is estimated based on U.S. 3-Month Treasury bills. *SR* of *BE 500* is computed as the ratio of the average excess return on *BE 500* over the average risk-free rate (*BE 500-RF*) to the standard deviation of the excess return s(*BE 500-RF*). Stock portfolios are formed based on the maximisation of the *FUN* of all stocks of *BE 500*. The dotted line in Figure a) shows the trend line of changes in the differences between the average return on *AvPOR* and the average return on the *BE 500* index. The dotted line in Figure c) shows the trend line of changes in the differences between the *SR* of *AvPOR* (*SR(AvPOR)*) and the *SR* of the *BE 500* index (*SR(BE 500)*). The analysed historical period from May 2001 through March 2022, 251 months.

Source: Own research.

Figure 5.9 illustrates the SARIMA model used to predict rolling differences between the 96-month average returns and SRs for the formed portfolios and the BE 500 index.

In Table A.4 (provided in the Appendix), we present the key parameters of the applied SARIMA model. Using the available data, we calculate confidence intervals for the forecasts of the differences in returns and SRs as of Q2 2009.

The SARIMA model reveals that the confidence interval for the forecasted differences in SRs (SR96) contains zero starting from Q2 2010 in most cases (see Figure 5.9b). Similar to the U.S. market, this suggests grounds for rejecting Conjecture 2 for the European market. Furthermore, the market's shift towards efficiency is also reflected in the return differences (see Figure 5.9a), supporting the rejection of Conjecture 1.

Figure 5.10 presents the Holt–Winters method used to predict rolling differences between the 96-month average returns and SRs for the formed portfolios and the BE 500 index.

In Table A.5 (Appendix), we present the key parameters of the Holt–Winters method. The results show that the confidence interval for the forecasted differences in SRs96 includes zero from Q3 2010 in most cases (see Figure 5.10b). The conclusions are consistent with those derived from the SARIMA model for this market, leading to the rejection of Conjecture 2. Similarly, the market's movement towards efficiency is evidenced by the differences in returns (see Figure 5.10a), supporting the rejection of Conjecture 1. These findings align with the results obtained using the SARIMA model.

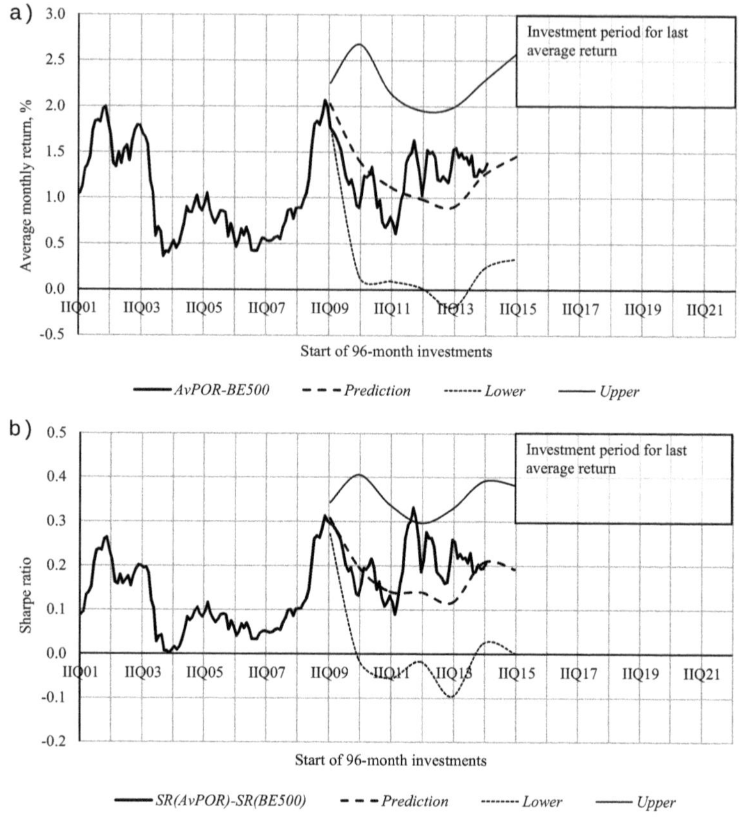

Figure 5.9 SARIMA and prediction of rolling differences between a) the 96-month average returns, b) SR on 96 months, corresponding to the formed portfolios and the values of *BE 500* index.

Notes: Each point of the chart presents the examined portfolio characteristics (average return and SR) at the beginning of the 96-month investment period. SR is computed as the ratio of the average excess return from the examined portfolio over the average risk-free rate (*Rp-RF*) to the standard deviation of the excess return s(*Rp-RF*). *RF* is estimated based on U.S. 3-Month Treasury bills. *AvPOR* is a linearly weighted portfolio consisting of 15, 10, 7, and 5 stock portfolios formed on *BE 500* index. Stock portfolios are formed based on the maximisation of the *FUN* of all stock of *BE 500*. The dashed thin top and bottom lines are the upper and lower bounds of the forecast confidence intervals. The dashed thick line represents the forecast values of the rolling return difference – in Figure a), and SR difference – in Figure b). The analysed historical period from May 2001 through March 2022, 251 months.

Source: Own research using R-Studio ver. 4.2.3.

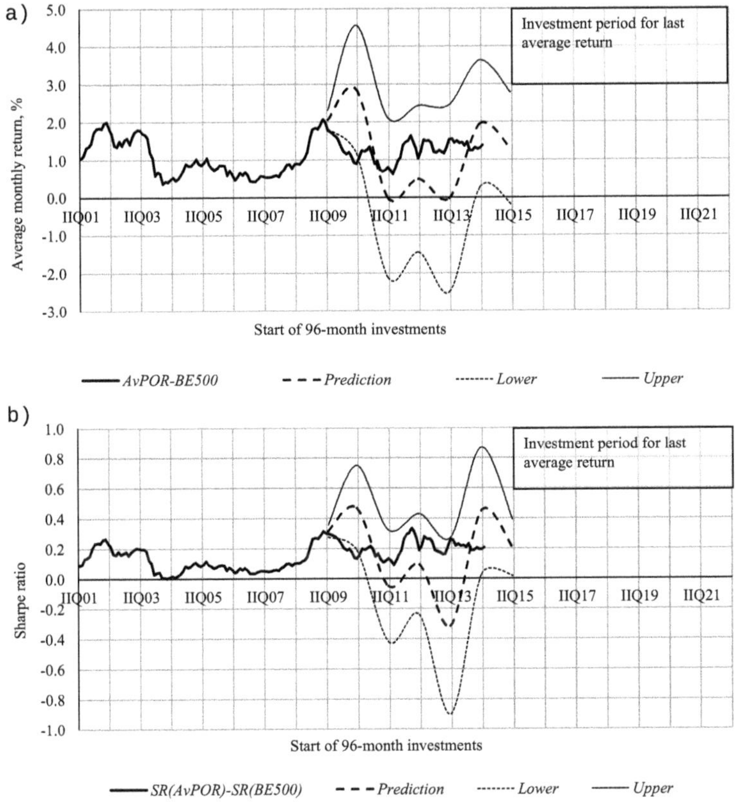

Figure 5.10 Holt–Winters method to predict rolling differences between a) the 96-month average returns, b) SR on 96 months, corresponding to the formed portfolios and the values of *BE 500* index.

Notes: Each point of the chart presents the examined portfolio characteristics (average return and SR) at the beginning of the 96-month investment period. SR is computed as the ratio of the average excess return from the examined portfolio over the average risk-free rate (*Rp-RF*) to the standard deviation of the excess return s(*Rp-RF*). *RF* is estimated based on U.S. 3-Month Treasury bills. *AvPOR* is a linearly weighted portfolio consisting of 15, 10, 7, and 5 stock portfolios formed on *BE 500* index. Stock portfolios are formed based on the maximisation of the *FUN* of all stocks of *BE 500*. The dashed thin top and bottom lines are the upper and lower bounds of the forecast confidence intervals. The dashed thick line represents the forecast values of the rolling return difference – in Figure a), and SR difference – in Figure b). The analysed historical period from May 2001 through March 2022, 251 months.

Source: Own research using ITSM ver. 7.1.

Figure 5.11 illustrates the SARIMA model's prediction of rolling differences between the 60-month average returns and SRs for the portfolios and the BE 500 index.

In Table A.6 (Appendix), we provide the key parameters of the SARIMA model. Available data are used to calculate confidence intervals for the forecasted differences in returns and SRs from Q2 2006 onwards. The SARIMA model indicates that the confidence interval for the forecasted differences in SRs60 contains zero from Q2 2006 in most cases (see Figure 5.11b). As with the U.S. market, this suggests grounds for rejecting Conjecture 2 for the European market. Furthermore, the market's progression towards efficiency is reflected in the differences in returns (see Figure 5.11a), leading to the rejection of Conjecture 1.

Figure 5.12 presents the Holt–Winters method's prediction of rolling differences between the 60-month average returns and SRs for the portfolios and the BE 500 index.

In Table A.7 (Appendix), we outline the key parameters of the Holt–Winters method. The results indicate that the confidence interval for the forecasted differences in SRs60 contains zero from Q2 2006 in most cases (see Figure 5.12b). The conclusions mirror those drawn from the SARIMA model for this market, leading to the rejection of Conjecture 2. Similarly, the market's move towards efficiency is again illustrated by the differences in returns (see Figure 5.12a), further supporting the rejection of Conjecture 1. These results are consistent with those obtained using the SARIMA model.

5.3 Japanese market

Figure 5.13 presents rolling 96-month average returns (a), rolling correlations between 96-month returns of the formed portfolio and the TOPIX 500 index (b), rolling SR of 96-month TOPIX 500 average portfolios (formed using the 5, 7, 10, and 15 highest FUN values) and the TOPIX 500 index (c), and rolling correlations between the SRs of these portfolios and the TOPIX 500 index (d). The correlations are calculated using 36-month windows.

The curves for returns and SRs depict the temporal changes in the formed portfolios and the index. The maximum average returns on 96-month investments in portfolios consisting of the top 5, 7, 10, and 15 companies (based on FUN values) from 2004 to 2022 were 22.7%, 24.3%, 23.0%, and 23.5%, respectively (annualised). Conversely, the minimum average returns for the same portfolios were 12.0%, 11.8%,

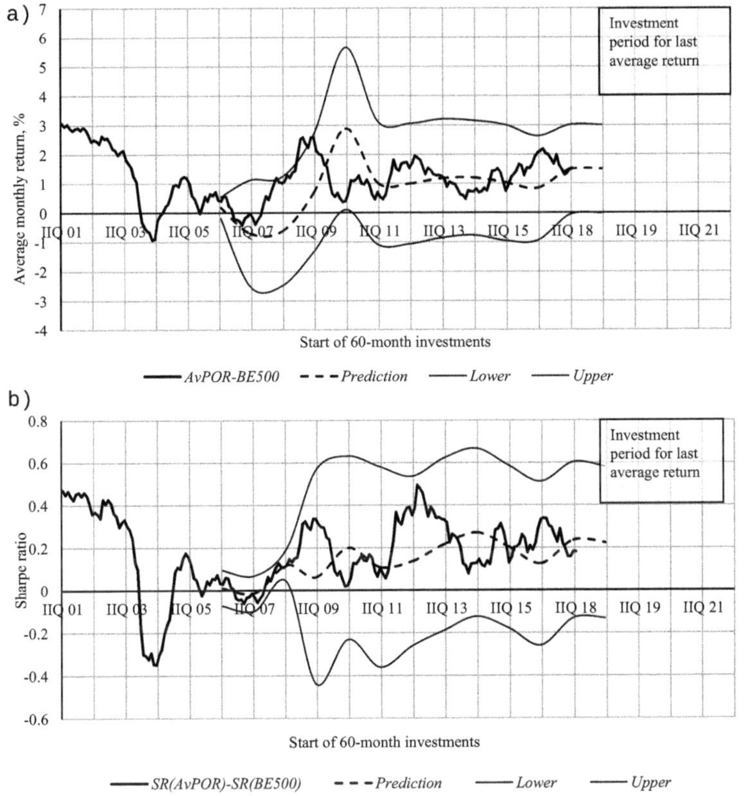

Figure 5.11 SARIMA and prediction of rolling differences between a) the 60-month average returns, b) SR on 60 months, corresponding to the formed portfolios and the values of *BE 500* index.

Notes: Each point of the chart presents the examined portfolio characteristics (average return and SR) at the beginning of the 60-month investment period. SR is computed as the ratio of the average excess return from the examined portfolio over the average risk-free rate (*Rp-RF*) to the standard deviation of the excess return s(*Rp-RF*). *RF* is estimated based on U.S. 3-Month Treasury bills. *AvPOR* is a linearly weighted portfolio consisting of 15, 10, 7, and 5 stock portfolios formed on *BE 500* index. Stock portfolios are formed based on the maximisation of the *FUN* of all stocks of *BE 500*. The dashed thin top and bottom lines are the upper and lower bounds of the forecast confidence intervals. The dashed thick line represents the forecast values of the rolling return difference – in Figure a), and SR difference – in Figure b). The analysed historical period from May 2001 through March 2022, 251 months.

Source: Own research using R-Studio ver. 4.2.3.

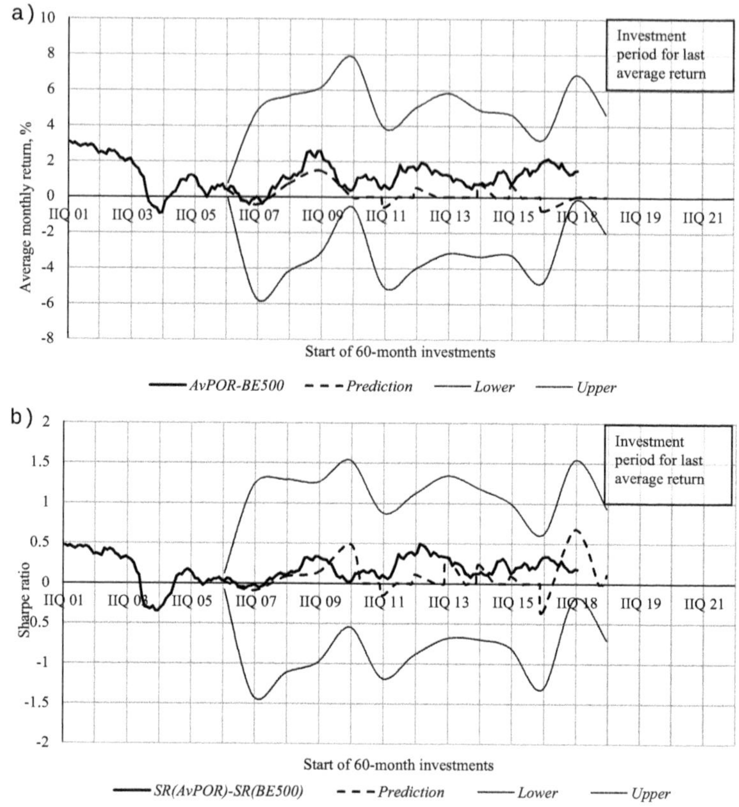

Figure 5.12 Holt–Winters method to predict rolling differences between a) the 60-month average returns, b) SR on 60 months, corresponding to the formed portfolios and the values of *BE 500* index.

Notes: Each point of the chart presents the examined portfolio characteristics (average return and SR) at the beginning of the 60-month investment period. SR is computed as the ratio of the average excess return from the examined portfolio over the average risk-free rate (*Rp-RF*) to the standard deviation of the excess return s(*Rp-RF*). *RF* is estimated based on U.S. 3-Month Treasury bills. *AvPOR* is a linearly weighted portfolio consisting of 15, 10, 7, and 5 stock portfolios formed on *BE 500* index. Stock portfolios are formed based on the maximisation of the *FUN* of all stock of *BE 500*. The dashed thin top and bottom lines are the upper and lower bounds of the forecast confidence intervals. The dashed thick line represents the forecast values of the rolling return difference – in Figure a), and SR difference – in Figure b). The analysed historical period from May 2001 through March 2022, 251 months.

Source: Own research using ITSM ver. 7.1.

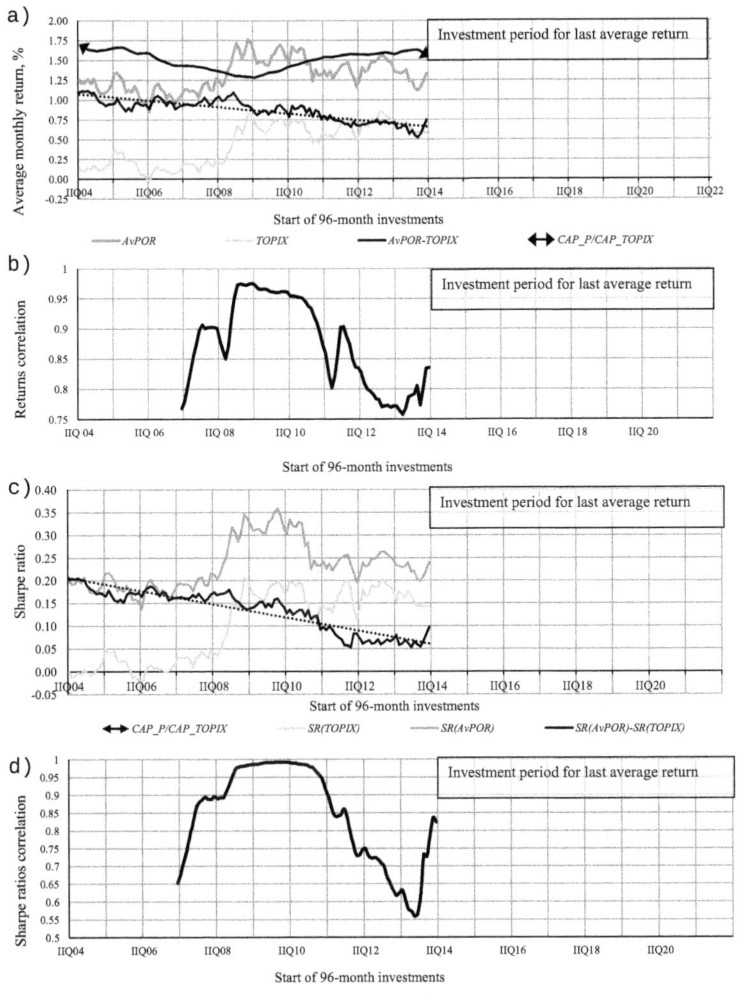

Figure 5.13 Rolling a) 96-month average returns, b) correlations between 96-month average returns of formed portfolio and the *TOPIX 500* index, c) *SR* on 96 months: of *TOPIX 500* formed portfolio and *TOPIX 500* index, d) correlations between *SR* of *TOPIX 500* formed portfolio and *TOPIX 500* index.

Notes: *AvPOR* is a linearly weighted portfolio consisting of 15, 10, 7, and 5 stock portfolios formed on *TOPIX 500* index. Each point of the chart represents the examined portfolio characteristics [average return, correlations between *AvPOR* and *TOPIX 500*

Figure 5.13 (Continued)

averaged returns, *SR*, correlations between *SR* of *AvPOR* and *SR* of *TOPIX 500* index, and ratio of 15 companies portfolio capitalisation (*CAP_P*) to the capitalisation of 50 companies with the maximum capitalisation of the index (*CAP_ TOPIX*)] at the beginning of the 96-month investment period. *SR* of *AvPOR* is computed as the ratio of the average excess return on *AvPOR* over the average risk-free rate (*AvPOR-RF*) to the standard deviation of the excess return s(*AvPOR-RF*). *RF* is estimated based on U.S. 3-Month Treasury bills. *SR* of *TOPIX 500* is computed as the ratio of the average excess return on *TOPIX 500* over the average risk-free rate (*TOPIX 500-RF*) to the standard deviation of the excess return s(*TOPIX 500-RF*). Stock portfolios are formed based on the maximisation of the *FUN* of all stocks of *TOPIX 500*. The dotted line in Figure a) shows the trend line of changes in the differences between the average return on *AvPOR* and the average return on the *TOPIX 500* index. The dotted line in Figure c) shows the trend line of changes in the differences between the *SR* of *AvPOR* (*SR(AvPOR)*) and the *SR* of the *TOPIX 500* index (*SR(TOPIX)*). The analysed historical period from May 2004 through March 2022, 215 months.

Source: Own research.

9.5%, and 9.6%, respectively. The maximum and minimum average returns for the average portfolio (comprising the 5, 7, 10, and 15-company portfolios) during the same period were 23.4% and 10.7%, respectively. The corresponding maximum and minimum average returns for the TOPIX 500 index were 10.8% and -0.4%, respectively.

An examination of these figures reveals significant differences between the returns of the formed portfolios and the index portfolio. However, the trend line of return differences steadily declines from approximately 1% to 0.7% per month. Similarly, for the SR, the trend line decreases from 0.22 to 0.05 (see Figures 5.13a and 5.13c).

A sharp increase in the correlation coefficient for returns between the formed portfolios and the TOPIX 500 index was observed between 2007 and 2009, rising from around 0.75 to 0.95. After this period, the correlation remained stable until 2011 and subsequently decreased to about 0.8. A similar pattern of change was noted for the correlation of the SRs between the formed portfolios and the TOPIX 500 index throughout the 2004–2022 period (see Figures 5.13b and 5.13d).

In contrast to the U.S. market, the relative capitalisation of the FUN-formed portfolio fluctuated between 1.25% and 1.75%, indicating that the 15 companies with the highest FUN values had relatively smaller capitalisations (in relation to the TOPIX 500 index) compared to their U.S. counterparts.

Figure 5.14 displays rolling 60-month average returns (a), rolling correlations between 60-month returns of the formed portfolios and the TOPIX 500 index (b), rolling SRs for the same portfolios and the

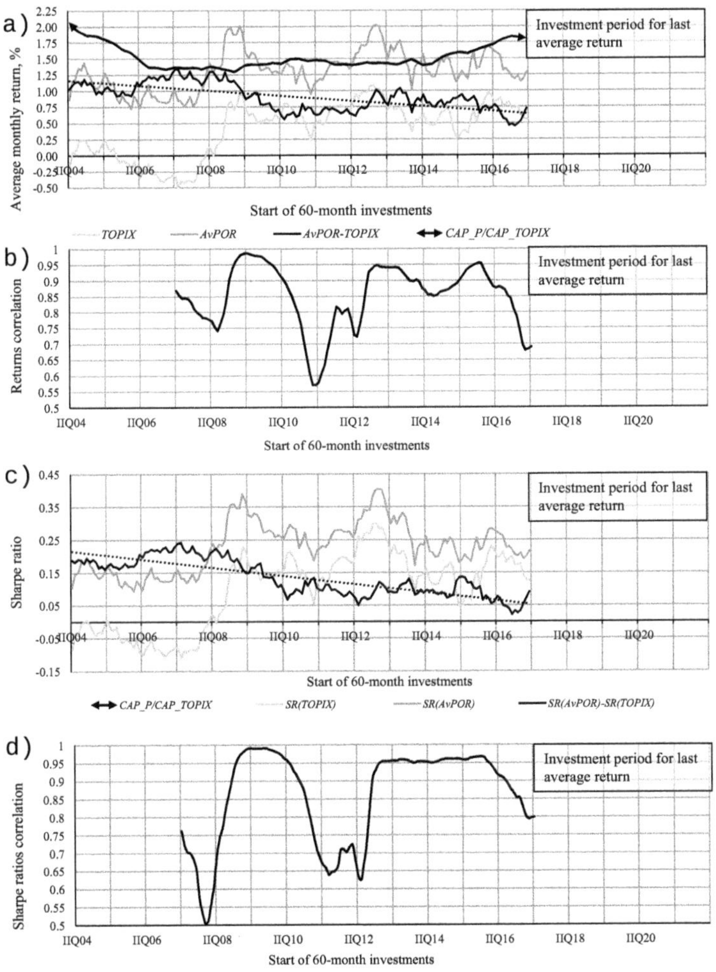

Figure 5.14 Rolling a) 60-month average returns, b) correlations between 60-month average returns of formed portfolio and the *TOPIX 500* index, c) *SR* on 60 months: of *TOPIX 500* formed portfolio and *TOPIX 500* index, d) correlations between the *SR* of *TOPIX 500* formed portfolio and *TOPIX 500* index.

Notes: *AvPOR* is a linearly weighted portfolio consisting of 15, 10, 7, and 5 stock portfolios formed on *TOPIX 500* index. Each point of the chart represents the examined portfolio characteristics [average return, correlations between *AvPOR* and *TOPIX 500* averaged returns, *SR*, correlations between *SR* of *AvPOR* and *SR* of *TOPIX 500* index,

Figure 5.14 (Continued)

and the ratio of 15 companies portfolio capitalisation (*CAP_P*) to the capitalisation of 50 companies with the maximum capitalisation of the index (*CAP_ TOPIX*)] at the beginning of the 60-month investment period. *SR* of *AvPOR* is computed as the ratio of the average excess return on *AvPOR* over the average risk-free rate (*AvPOR-RF*) to the standard deviation of the excess return s(*AvPOR-RF*). *RF* is estimated based on U.S. 3-Month Treasury bills. *SR* of *TOPIX 500* is computed as the ratio of the average excess return on *TOPIX 500* over the average risk-free rate (*TOPIX 500-RF*) to the standard deviation of the excess return s(*TOPIX 500-RF*). Stock portfolios are formed based on the maximisation of the *FUN* of all stocks of *TOPIX 500*. The dotted line in Figure a) shows the trend line of changes in the differences between the average return on *AvPOR* and the average return on the *TOPIX 500* index. The dotted line in Figure c) shows the trend line of changes in the differences between the *SR* of *AvPOR* (*SR(AvPOR)*) and the *SR* of the *TOPIX 500* index (*SR(TOPIX)*). The analysed historical period from May 2004 through March 2022, 215 months.

Source: Own research.

TOPIX 500 index (c), and rolling correlations between their SRs (d). Again, the correlations are calculated using 36-month windows.

The curves for returns and SRs illustrate changes over time for the formed portfolios and the index. The maximum average returns on 60-month investments in the top 5, 7, 10, and 15 portfolios (based on the highest FUN values) during the 2004–2022 period were 22.7%, 28.5%, 27.4%, and 28.5%, respectively (annualised). The minimum returns for these portfolios were 10.1%, 12.0%, 7.2%, and 5.1%, respectively. The maximum and minimum average returns for the average portfolio over the same period were 28.1% and 8.6%, respectively, while for the TOPIX 500 index, these values were 13.8% and -5.8%, respectively.

A careful review of these figures indicates considerable differences between the returns of the formed portfolios and the index. As with the 96-month analysis, the trend line of return differences declines from approximately 1.1% to 0.7% per month, and the SR trend line drops from 0.22 to 0.05 (see Figures 5.14a and 5.14c).

The correlation coefficient for returns between the formed portfolios and the TOPIX 500 index also increased significantly between 2007 and 2009, from about 0.75 to 0.95. After this, the correlation stabilised until 2010, before decreasing to roughly 0.5 in the subsequent years. A similar pattern was observed in the correlation of SRs between the formed portfolios and the TOPIX 500 index throughout the 2004–2022 period (see Figures 5.14b and 5.14d).

In contrast to the U.S. market, the relative capitalisation of the FUN-formed portfolio ranged between 1.30% and 2.00%, suggesting that the companies with the highest FUN values have relatively smaller capitalisations compared to the TOPIX 500 index, similar to the previous analysis.

Using similar methodologies to those employed for the U.S. and European markets, we examine the time series of the differences between the return values (AvPOR-TOPIX) and SRs (SR(AvPOR)-SR(TOPIX)) of the formed portfolios and the index.

Figure 5.15 illustrates the SARIMA model's predictions for rolling differences between 96-month average returns and SRs for the formed portfolios and the TOPIX 500 index.

Table A.8 (provided in the Appendix) presents the key parameters of the applied SARIMA model. Most of the analysed models display statistically significant parameters. The available data for the Japanese market allow forecasting from Q2 2012 onwards.

Despite the downward trend in SR differences throughout the tested period (see Figure 5.13c), the confidence interval generated by the SARIMA model does not include zero values (see Figure 5.15b). A similar pattern applies to the return differences (see Figure 5.13a). Thus, we conclude that there are no grounds to reject Conjectures 1 and 2 for the 2004–2022 period, which distinguishes the Japanese market from the U.S. and European markets.

Figure 5.16 shows the Holt–Winters method's predictions for rolling differences between 96-month average returns and SRs for the formed portfolios and the TOPIX 500 index.

Table A.9 (provided in the Appendix) presents key parameters for the applied Holt–Winters method.

The Holt–Winters method reveals that the confidence intervals for forecasted SR differences (for starting investment) contain zero from Q2 2013 to Q2 2014 (see Figure 5.16b). However, more recent forecasts indicate that, from Q2 2014 onward, the confidence interval for the SR differences no longer contains zero. Consequently, across the period from Q2 2004 to Q2 2022, there is insufficient evidence to reject Conjecture 2. Regarding average return differences, the calculated confidence interval does not contain zero (for starting investment) from Q2 2012 to Q2 2015, further supporting the retention of Conjecture 1.

Figure 5.17 illustrates the SARIMA model used to predict rolling differences between the 60-month average returns and SRs, corresponding to the formed portfolios and the TOPIX 500 index.

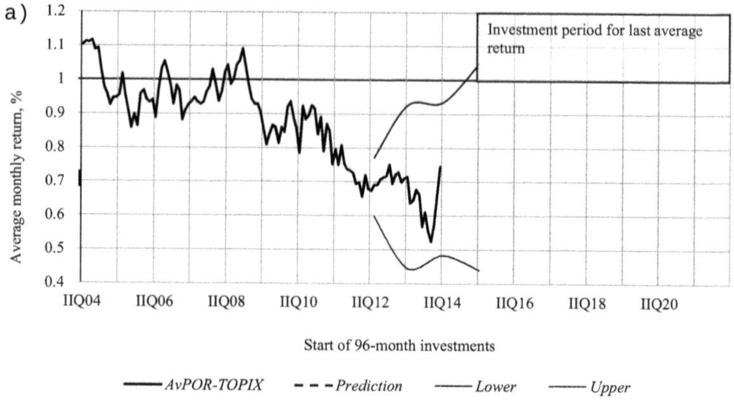

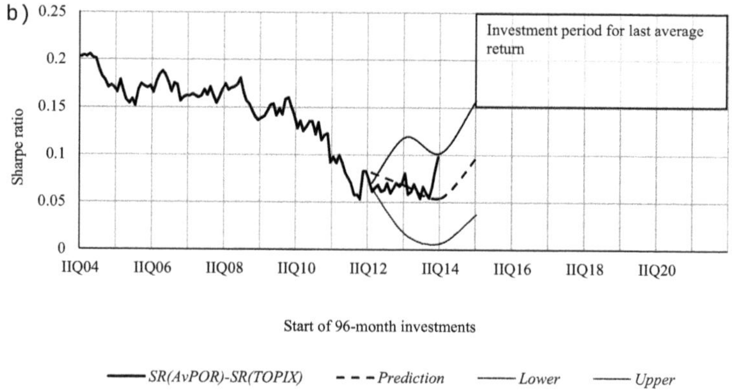

Figure 5.15 SARIMA and prediction of rolling differences between a) 96-month average returns, b) *SR* on 96 months, corresponding to the formed portfolios and the values of *TOPIX 500* index.

Notes: Each point of the chart presents the examined portfolio characteristics (average return and *SR*) at the beginning of the 96-month investment period. *SR* is computed as the ratio of the average excess return from the examined portfolio over the average risk-free rate (*Rp-RF*) to the standard deviation of the excess return s(*Rp-RF*). *RF* is estimated based on U.S. 3-Month Treasury bills. *AvPOR* is a linearly weighted portfolio consisting of 15, 10, 7, and 5 stock portfolios formed on *TOPIX 500* index. Stock portfolios are formed based on the maximisation of the *FUN* of all stocks of *TOPIX 500*. The dashed thin top and bottom lines are the upper and lower bounds of the forecast confidence intervals. The dashed thick line represents the forecast values of the rolling return difference – in Figure a), and *SR* difference – in Figure b). The analysed historical period from May 2004 through March 2022, 215 months.

Source: Own research using R-Studio ver. 4.2.3.

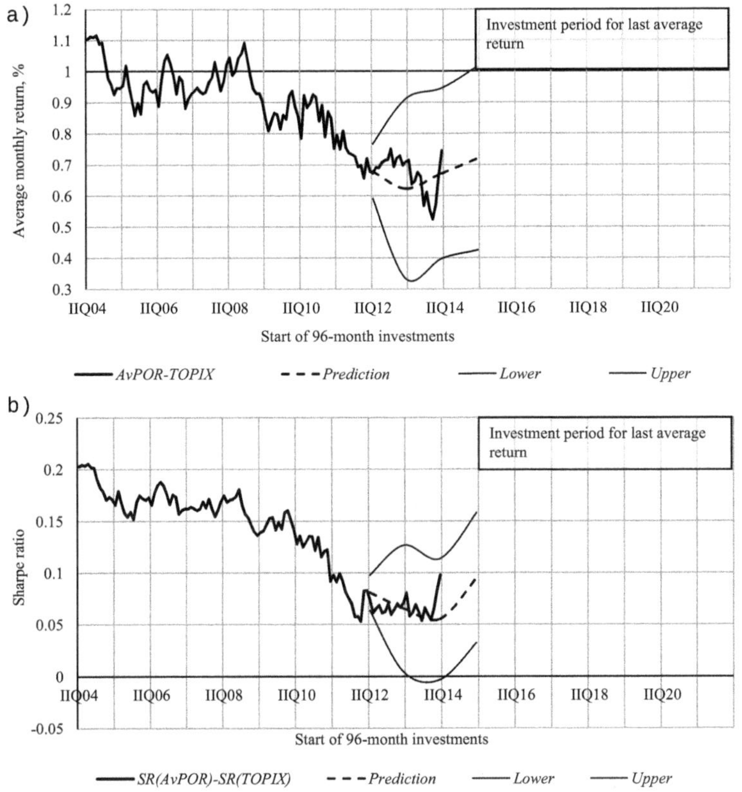

Figure 5.16 Holt–Winters method to predict rolling differences between a) the 96-month average returns, b) *SR* on 96 months, corresponding to the formed portfolios and the values of *TOPIX 500* index.

Notes: Each point of the chart presents the examined portfolio characteristics (average return and *SR*) at the beginning of the 96-month investment period. *SR* is computed as the ratio of the average excess return from the examined portfolio over the average risk-free rate (*Rp-RF*) to the standard deviation of the excess return s(*Rp-RF*). *RF* is estimated based on U.S. 3-Month Treasury bills. *AvPOR* is a linearly weighted portfolio consisting of 15, 10, 7, and 5 stock portfolios formed on *TOPIX 500* index. Stock portfolios are formed based on the maximisation of the *FUN* of all stocks of *TOPIX 500*. The dashed thin top and bottom lines are the upper and lower bounds of the forecast confidence intervals. The dashed thick line represents the forecast values of the rolling return difference – in Figure a), and *SR* difference – in Figure b). The analysed historical period from May 2004 through March 2022, 215 months.

Source: Own research using ITSM ver. 7.1.

Table A.10 (provided in the Appendix) provides the key parameters of the applied SARIMA model.

Most of the analysed models exhibit statistically significant parameters. For the Japanese market, the available data permit forecasting starting from Q2 2009. The confidence interval generated by the SARIMA model contains zero for SR values between Q3 2012 and Q2 2015 (see Figure 5.17b). However, the structure of changes in return differences leads to a different pattern. The confidence interval across the entire range of changes remains above zero (see Figure 5.17a). Therefore, it can be concluded that, for the entire period from 2004 to 2022, there is no basis to reject Conjectures 1 and 2. This contrasts sharply with the U.S. and European markets.

Figure 5.18 illustrates the Holt–Winters method's predictions of rolling differences between the 60-month average returns and SRs, corresponding to the formed portfolios and the TOPIX 500 index.

Table A.11 (provided in the Appendix) presents key parameters for the applied Holt–Winters method. The confidence interval generated by the Holt–Winters method contains zero SR values from Q2 2010 to Q3 2015 and from Q3 2016 onwards (see Figure 5.18b). A slightly different structure is observed when considering return differences, with the confidence interval containing zero values between Q2 2010 and Q3 2013 (see Figure 5.18a). Thus, it can be concluded that, between Q2 2010 and Q3 2013, there is sufficient evidence to reject Conjectures 1 and 2. This further highlights the stark contrast between the Japanese market and the U.S. and European markets.

5.4 Chinese market

Figure 5.19 presents the rolling 96-month average returns (a), rolling correlations between the 96-month formed portfolio and the SSE 380 average returns (b), rolling SRs for 96-month SSE 380 average portfolios (formed from the 5, 7, 10, and 15 companies with the highest FUN values) and the SSE 380 index (c), as well as the rolling correlations between the SRs of the SSE 380 portfolios and the SSE 380 index (d). The correlations are calculated using 36-month windows.

The curves representing the time series of returns and SRs illustrate changes over time for the formed portfolios and the entire index. The maximum average returns for 96-month investments in the portfolios of the 5, 7, 10, and 15 companies (with the highest FUN values) from

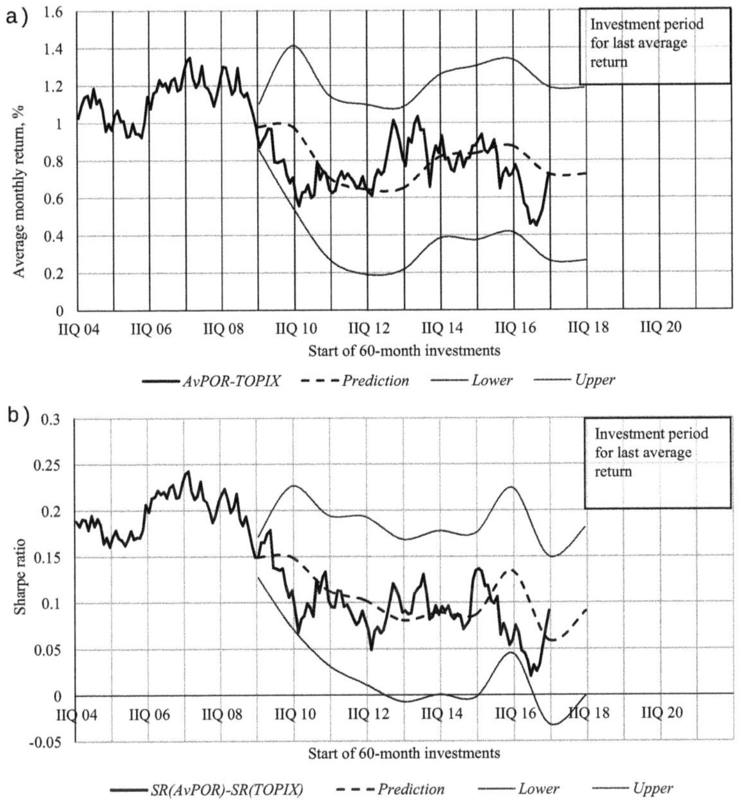

Figure 5.17 SARIMA and prediction of rolling differences between a) 60-month average returns, b) *SR* on 60 months, corresponding to the formed portfolios and the values of *TOPIX 500* index.

Notes: Each point of the chart presents the examined portfolio characteristics (average return and *SR*) at the beginning of the 60-month investment period. *SR* is computed as the ratio of the average excess return from the examined portfolio over the average risk-free rate (*Rp-RF*) to the standard deviation of the excess return s(*Rp-RF*). *RF* is estimated based on U.S. 3-Month Treasury bills. *AvPOR* is a linearly weighted portfolio consisting of 15, 10, 7, and 5 stock portfolios formed on *TOPIX 500* index. Stock portfolios are formed based on the maximisation of the *FUN* of all stocks of *TOPIX 500*. The dashed thin top and bottom lines are the upper and lower bounds of the forecast confidence intervals. The dashed thick line represents the forecast values of the rolling return difference – in Figure a), and *SR* difference – in Figure b). The analysed historical period from May 2004 through March 2022, 215 months.

Source: Own research using R-Studio ver. 4.2.3.

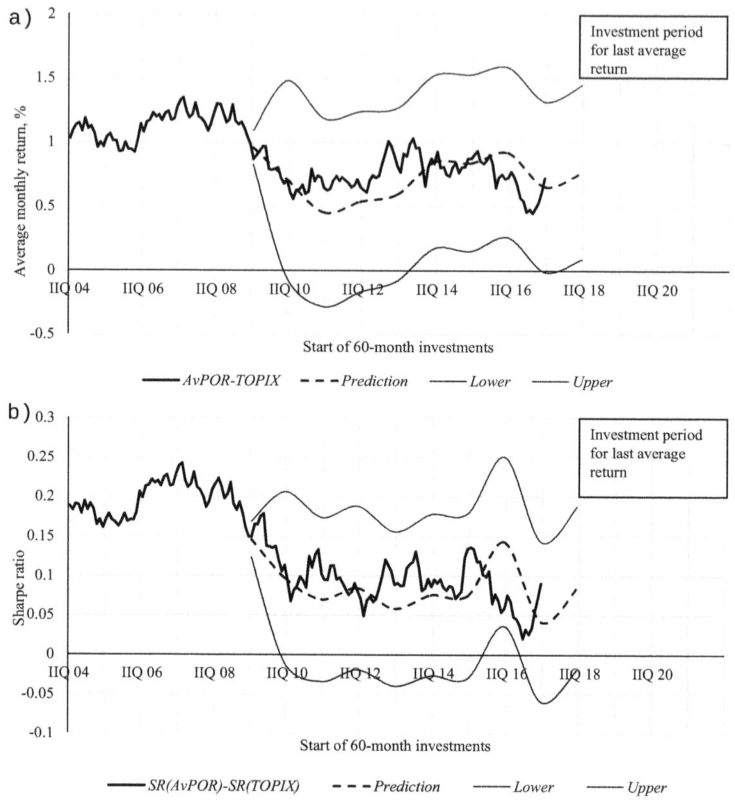

Figure 5.18 Holt–Winters method to predict rolling differences between a) the 60-month average returns, b) *SR* on 60 months, corresponding to the formed portfolios and the values of *TOPIX 500* index.

Notes: Each point of the chart presents the examined portfolio characteristics (average return and *SR*) at the beginning of the 60-month investment period. *SR* is computed as the ratio of the average excess return from the examined portfolio over the average risk-free rate (*Rp-RF*) to the standard deviation of the excess return s(*Rp-RF*). *RF* is estimated based on U.S. 3-Month Treasury bills. *AvPOR* is a linearly weighted portfolio consisting of 15, 10, 7, and 5 stock portfolios formed on *TOPIX 500* index. Stock portfolios are formed based on the maximisation of the *FUN* of all stocks of *TOPIX 500*. The dashed thin top and bottom lines are the upper and lower bounds of the forecast confidence intervals. The dashed thick line represents the forecast values of the rolling return difference – in Figure a), and *SR* difference – in Figure b). The analysed historical period from May 2004 through March 2022, 215 months.

Source: Own research using ITSM ver. 7.1.

2003 to 2022 are 41.9%, 43.3%, 47.4%, and 44.6% per year, respectively. The minimum average returns for the same portfolios over this period are 17.2%, 20.1%, 21.4%, and 19.3% per year, respectively.

The maximum and minimum average returns for 96-month investments in the average portfolio (comprising the portfolios of 5, 7, 10, and 15 companies) between 2003 and 2022 are 44.3% and 19.5% per year, respectively. The maximum and minimum average returns for 96-month investments in the SSE 380 index during the same period are 34.5% and 2.58% per year, respectively.

A careful examination of these figures reveals significant differences between the returns of the formed portfolios and those of the index from 2007 onwards. These differences were relatively smaller between 2003 and 2007, which is also reflected in the SR data. The characteristic trend lines for these differences show an increase from approximately 0% to 1.5% for average returns and from 0 to 0.15 for SRs (see Figures 5.19a and 5.19c).

The most pronounced changes in the correlation coefficient of returns (between the formed portfolios and the SSE 380 index) occurred between 2008 and 2012. In 2008, the correlation fell from about 0.95 to 0.65, and in 2011 it rose again to 0.9 before dropping back to 0.65. Similar fluctuations in the correlation of the SRs are evident throughout the 2003–2022 period (see Figures 5.19b and 5.19d).

Changes in the ratio of the average portfolio capitalisation to the average capitalisation of the 50 largest companies in the index suggest that the relative capitalisation of the portfolio decreased from 2003 to 2007, with values ranging from approximately 13% to 3%. This trend may partly explain the smaller differences between the returns of the formed portfolios and the index up to 2007.

Figure 5.20 presents the rolling 60-month average returns (a), rolling correlations between the 60-month formed portfolio and SSE 380 average returns (b), rolling SRs for 60-month SSE 380 average portfolios (formed from the 5, 7, 10, and 15 companies with the highest FUN values) and the SSE 380 index (c), as well as rolling correlations between the SRs of the SSE 380 portfolios and the SSE 380 index (d). The correlations are calculated using 36-month windows.

The curves for returns and SRs show temporal changes for the formed portfolios and the index. The maximum average returns for 60-month investments in the portfolios of 5, 7, 10, and 15 companies (with the highest FUN values) from 2003 to 2022 are 57.0%, 66.9%, 65.6%, and 73.1% per year, respectively. The minimum average

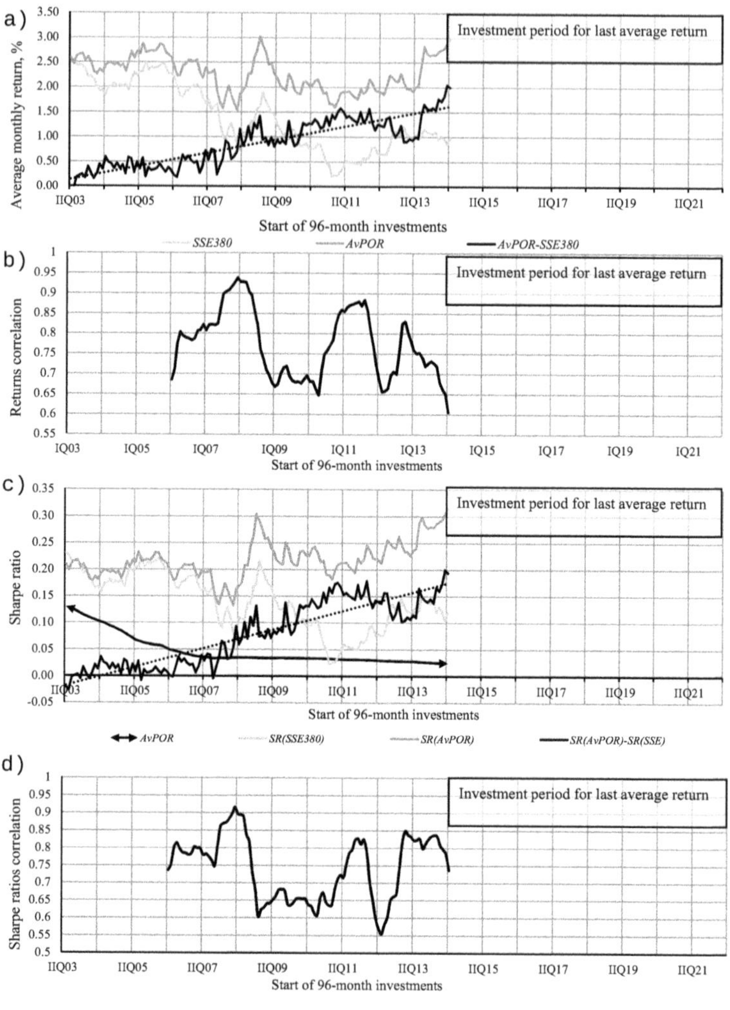

Figure 5.19 Rolling a) 96-month average returns, b) correlations between 96-month *SSE 380* formed portfolio and *SSE 380* index average returns, c) *SR* on 96 months: of *SSE 380* formed portfolio and *SSE 380* index, d) correlations between *SR* of *SSE 380* formed portfolio and *SSE 380* index.

Notes: *AvPOR* is a linearly weighted portfolio consisting of 15, 10, 7, and 5 stock portfolios formed on *SSE 380* index. Each point of the chart presents the examined portfolio characteristics [average return, correlations between *AvPOR* and *SSE 380* average

Figure 5.19 (Continued)

returns, *SR*, correlations between *SR* of *AvPOR* and *SR* of *SSE 380* index, and ratio of 15 companies portfolio capitalisation (*CAP_P*) to the capitalisation of 50 companies with the maximum capitalisation of the index (*CAP_SSE*))] at the beginning of the 96-month investment period. *SR* of *AvPOR* is computed as the ratio of the average excess return on *AvPOR* over the average risk-free rate (*AvPOR-RF*) to the standard deviation of the excess return s(*AvPOR-RF*). *RF* is estimated based on U.S. 3-Month Treasury bills. *SR* of *SSE 380* is computed as the ratio of the average excess return on *SSE 380* over the average risk-free rate (*SSE 380-RF*) to the standard deviation of the excess return s(*SSE 380-RF*). Stock portfolios are formed based on the maximisation of the *FUN* of all stocks of *SSE 380*. The dotted line in Figure a) shows the trend line of changes in the differences between the average return on *AvPOR* and the average return on the *SSE 380* index. The dotted line in Figure c) shows the trend lines of changes in the differences between the *SR* of *AvPOR* (*SR(AvPOR)*) and the *SR* of the *SSE 380* index (*SR(SSE)*). The analysed historical period from May 2003 through March 2022, 227 months.

Source: Own research.

returns for the same portfolios are 5.3%, 7.4%, 6.1%, and 7.6% per year, respectively.

The maximum and minimum average returns for 60-month investments in the average portfolio (comprising the portfolios of 5, 7, 10, and 15 companies) between 2003 and 2022 are 65.6% and 6.6% per year, respectively. The maximum and minimum average returns for 60-month investments in the SSE 380 index during the same period are 61.2% and -9.4% per year, respectively.

Analysis of these figures reveals that the differences between the returns of the formed portfolios and the index became more significant from 2011 onwards. Between 2003 and 2010, these differences were smaller, which is also visible in the SR data. The trend lines for the differences show an increase from around 0% to 2% for average returns and from -0.5 to approximately 0.2 for SRs (see Figures 5.20a and 5.20c).

The most significant changes in the correlation coefficient of returns (between the formed portfolios and the SSE 380 index) were observed between 2009 and 2015. In 2009, the correlation dropped from about 0.95 to 0.45, then increased to 0.94 in 2015 before falling again to 0.65. Similar variations in the correlation of SRs are seen throughout the analysed period (see Figures 5.20b and 5.20d).

Changes in the ratio of the average portfolio capitalisation to the average capitalisation of the 50 largest companies in the index indicate a decrease in the portfolio's relative capitalisation from 2003 to 2007, with values ranging from approximately 18% to 3%. This may partly explain the smaller differences between the returns of the formed portfolios and the index until 2007.

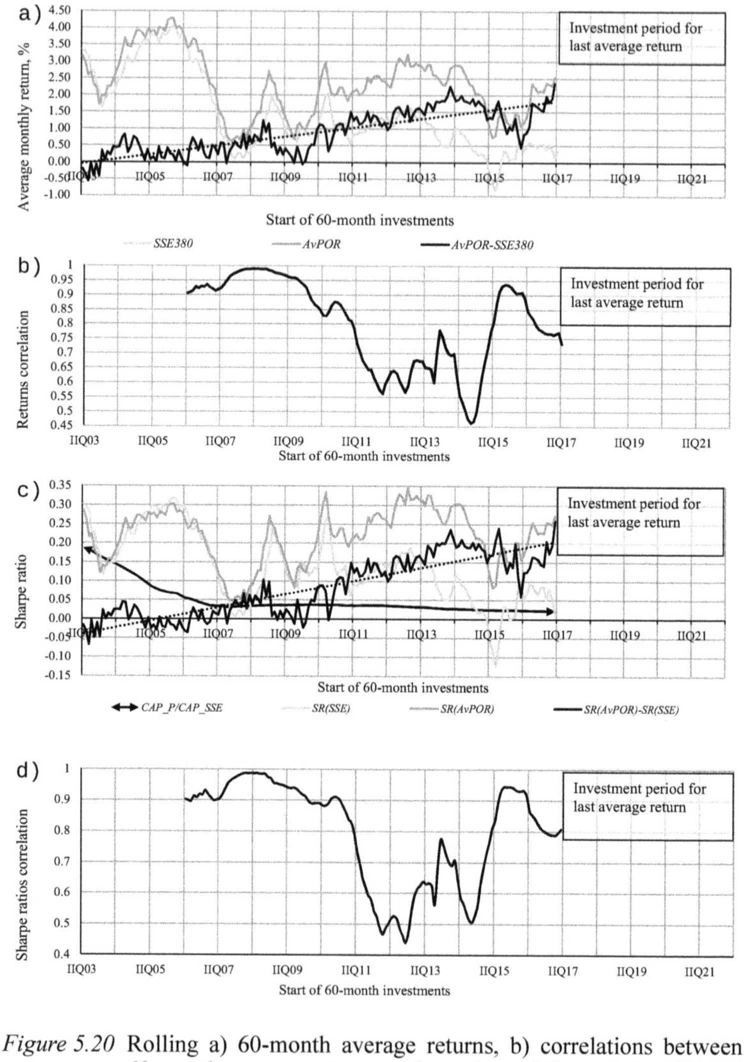

Figure 5.20 Rolling a) 60-month average returns, b) correlations between 60-month average returns of formed portfolio and the *SSE 380* index, c) *SR* on 60 months: of *SSE 380* formed portfolio and *SSE 380* index, d) correlations between the *SR* of *SSE 380* formed portfolio and *SSE 380* index.

Notes: *AvPOR* is a linearly weighted portfolio consisting of 15, 10, 7, and 5 stock portfolios formed on *SSE 380* index. Each point of the chart presents the examined

Figure 5.20 (Continued)

portfolio characteristics [average return, correlations between *AvPOR* and *SSE 380* average returns, *SR*, correlations between *SR* of *AvPOR* and *SR* of *SSE 380* index, and ratio of 15 companies portfolio capitalisation (*CAP_P*) to the capitalisation of 50 companies with the maximum capitalisation of the index (*CAP_SSE*))] at the beginning of the 96-month investment period. *SR* of *AvPOR* is computed as the ratio of the average excess return on *AvPOR* over the average risk-free rate (*AvPOR-RF*) to the standard deviation of the excess return s(*AvPOR-RF*). *RF* is estimated based on U.S. 3-Month Treasury bills. *SR* of *SSE 380* is computed as the ratio of the average excess return on *SSE 380* over the average risk-free rate (*SSE 380-RF*) to the standard deviation of the excess return s(*SSE 380-RF*). Stock portfolios are formed based on the maximisation of the *FUN* of all stocks of *SSE 380*. The dotted line in Figure a) shows the trend line of changes in the differences between the average return on *AvPOR* and the average return on the *SSE 380* index. The dotted line in Figure c) shows the trend lines of changes in the differences between the *SR* of *AvPOR* (*SR(AvPOR)*) and the *SR* of the *SSE 380* index (*SR(SSE)*). The analysed historical period from May 2003 through March 2022, 227 months.

Source: Own research.

Using the methods previously outlined, we now examine the time series differences between the returns of the average portfolio and the SSE 380 index (AvPOR-SSE), as well as the differences in the SRs (SR(AvPOR)-SR(SSE)).

Figure 5.21 shows the SARIMA model used to predict rolling differences between the 96-month average returns and SRs for the formed portfolios and the SSE 380 index.

Table A.12 (provided in the Appendix) presents the key parameters of the SARIMA model. Most of the models analysed exhibit statistically significant parameters. It should be noted that, for the Chinese market, available data permits forecasting from Q2 2011 onwards.

Unlike the U.S. and Japanese markets, the trend lines for return and SR differences in the Chinese market exhibit a positive slope. However, similar to the Japanese market, the confidence intervals generated by the SARIMA model do not include zero values (see Figures 5.21a and 5.21b). Therefore, it can be concluded that there is no basis to reject Conjectures 1 and 2.

Figure 5.22 presents the Holt–Winters method used to predict rolling differences between the 96-month average returns and SRs for the formed portfolios and the SSE 380 index.

Table A.13 (provided in the Appendix) presents the key parameters of the Holt–Winters model. The results from this method show that, for most of the periods studied, the confidence intervals for forecasted return and SR differences do not contain zero (see Figures 5.22a and

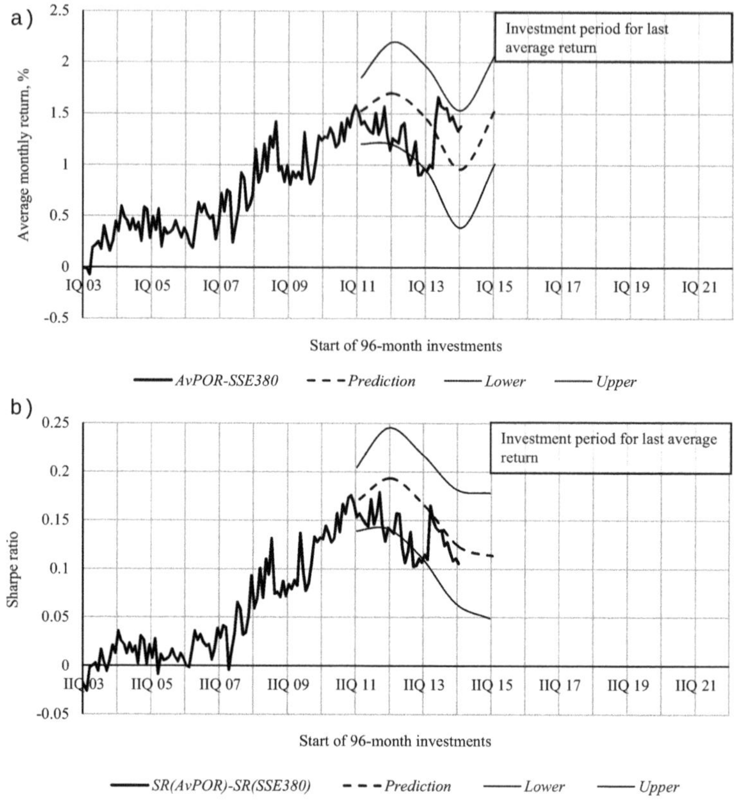

Figure 5.21 SARIMA and prediction of rolling differences between a) 96-month average returns, b) *SR* on 96 months, corresponding to the formed portfolios and the values of *SSE 380* index.

Notes: Each point of the chart presents the examined portfolio characteristics (average return and *SR*) at the beginning of the 96-month investment period. *SR* is computed as the ratio of the average excess return from the examined portfolio over the average risk-free rate (*Rp-RF*) to the standard deviation of the excess return s(*Rp-RF*). *RF* is estimated based on U.S. 3-Month Treasury bills. *AvPOR* is a linearly weighted portfolio consisting of 15, 10, 7, and 5 stock portfolios formed on *SSE 380* index. Stock portfolios are formed based on the maximisation of the *FUN* of all stocks of *SSE 380*. The dashed thin top and bottom lines are the upper and lower bounds of the forecast confidence intervals. The dashed thick line represents the forecast values of the rolling return difference – in Figure a), and *SR* difference – in Figure b). The analysed historical period from May 2003 through March 2022, 227 months.

Source: Own research using R-Studio ver. 4.2.3.

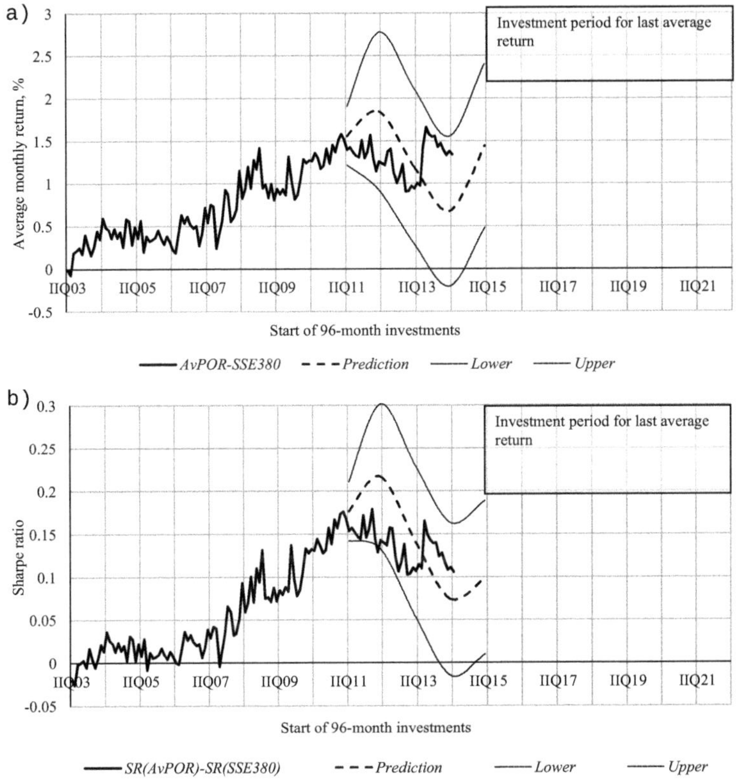

Figure 5.22 Holt–Winters method to predict rolling differences between a) 96-month average returns, b) *SR* on 96 months, corresponding to the formed portfolios and the values of *SSE 380* index.

Notes: Each point of the chart presents the examined portfolio characteristics (averaged return and *SR*) at the beginning of the 96-month investment period. *SR* is computed as the ratio of the average excess return from the examined portfolio over the average risk-free rate (*Rp-RF*) to the standard deviation of the excess return s(*Rp-RF*). *RF* is estimated based on U.S. 3-Month Treasury bills. *AvPOR* is a linearly weighted portfolio consisting of 15, 10, 7, and 5 stock portfolios formed on *SSE 380* index. Stock portfolios are formed based on the maximisation of the *FUN* of all stocks of tested indexes. The dashed thin top and bottom lines are the upper and lower bounds of the forecast confidence intervals. The dashed thick line represents the forecast values of the rolling return difference – in Figure a), and *SR* difference – in Figure b). The analysed historical period from May 2003 through March 2022, 227 months.

Source: Own research using ITSM ver. 7.1.

5.22b). Therefore, it can be concluded that there is no basis to reject Conjectures 1 and 2 in the investigated periods.

Figure 5.23 shows the SARIMA model used to predict rolling differences between the 60-month average returns and SRs for the formed portfolios and the SSE 380 index.

Table A.14 (provided in the Appendix) presents the key parameters of the SARIMA model. Available data were used to calculate confidence intervals for forecasts of return and SR differences starting from Q2 2008.

Unlike the U.S. and Japanese markets, the trend lines for return and SR differences in the Chinese market show a positive slope (see Figures 5.20a and 5.20c). However, the confidence intervals generated by the SARIMA model contain zero SR values for the periods from Q2 2008 to Q3 2011 and from Q1 2018 (see Figure 5.23b). Similar changes in the confidence interval values are observed for return differences (see Figure 5.23a). Therefore, it can be concluded that, for the periods from Q2 2008 to Q3 2011 and from Q1 2018, there is reason to reject Conjectures 2 and 1.

Figure 5.24 presents the Holt–Winters method used to predict rolling differences between the 60-month average returns and SRs for the formed portfolios and the SSE 380 index.

Table A.15 (provided in the Appendix) presents the key parameters of the Holt–Winters method. The confidence intervals generated by this method contain zero SR values for the periods from Q2 2009 to Q2 2012 and from Q1 2018 (see Figure 5.24b). Similar changes in the confidence intervals occur for return differences (see Figure 5.24a). Therefore, it can be concluded that, for the periods from Q2 2009 to Q2 2012 and from Q1 2018, there is reason to reject Conjectures 2 and 1. This highlights a stark contrast between the Chinese market and the U.S. and European markets.

5.5 Polish market

Figure 5.25 presents rolling average returns (a), rolling correlations between the formed portfolios and the WIG index average returns (b), rolling SR for 96-month periods of WIG average portfolios (formed from the 5, 7, 10, and 15 companies with the highest FUN values) and the WIG index (c), as well as rolling correlations between the SRs of WIG portfolios and the WIG index (d). The correlations are calculated using 36-month windows.

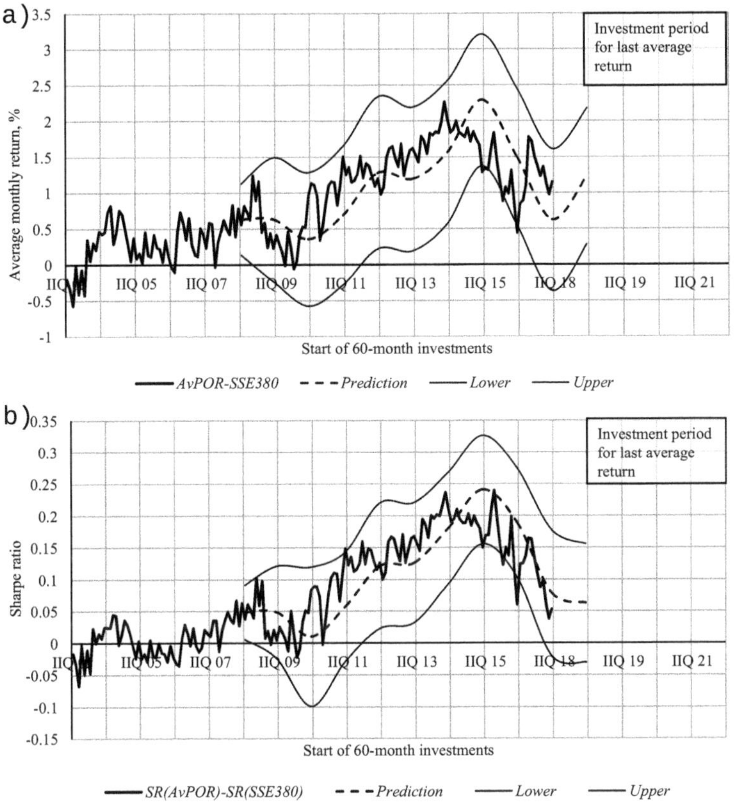

Figure 5.23 SARIMA and prediction of rolling differences between a) 60-month average returns, b) *SR* on 60 months, corresponding to the formed portfolios and the values of *SSE 380* index.

Notes: Each point of the chart presents the examined portfolio characteristics (average return and *SR*) at the beginning of the 60-month investment period. *SR* is computed as the ratio of the average excess return from the examined portfolio over the average risk-free rate (*Rp-RF*) to the standard deviation of the excess return s(*Rp-RF*). *RF* is estimated based on U.S. 3-Month Treasury bills. *AvPOR* is a linearly weighted portfolio consisting of 15, 10, 7, and 5 stock portfolios formed on *SSE 380* index. Stock portfolios are formed based on the maximisation of the *FUN* of all stocks of *SSE 380*. The dashed thin top and bottom lines are the upper and lower bounds of the forecast confidence intervals. The dashed thick line represents the forecast values of the rolling return difference – in Figure a), and *SR* difference – in Figure b). The analysed historical period from May 2003 through March 2022, 227 months.

Source: Own research using R-Studio ver. 4.2.3.

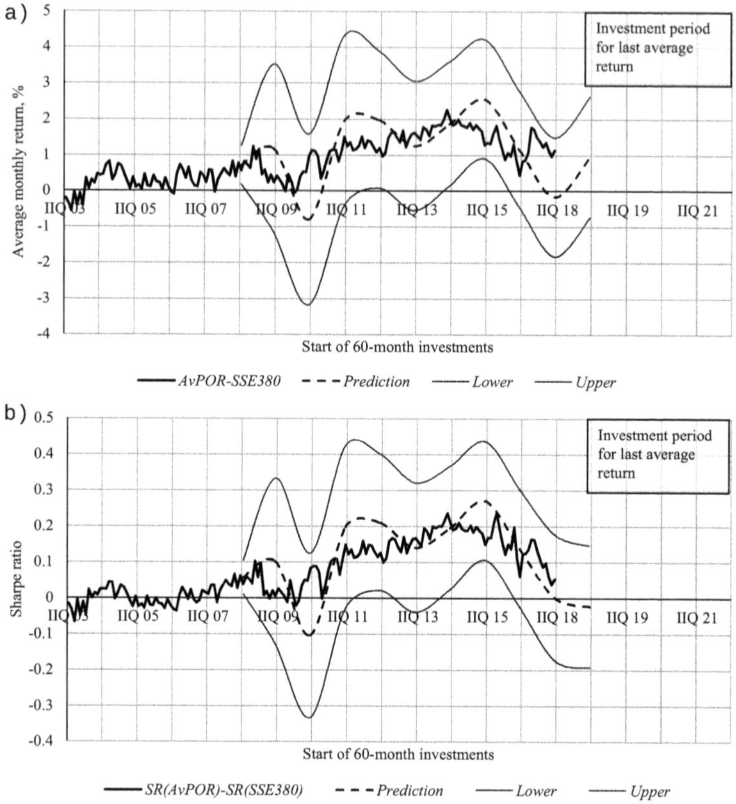

Figure 5.24 Holt–Winters method to predict rolling differences between a) 60-month average returns, b) *SR* on 96 months, corresponding to the formed portfolios and the values of *SSE 380* index.

Notes: Each point of the chart presents the examined portfolio characteristics (averaged return and *SR*) at the beginning of the 60-month investment period. *SR* is computed as the ratio of the average excess return from the examined portfolio over the average risk-free rate (*Rp-RF*) to the standard deviation of the excess return s(*Rp-RF*). *RF* is estimated based on U.S. 3-Month Treasury bills. *AvPOR* is a linearly weighted portfolio consisting of 15, 10, 7, and 5 stock portfolios formed on *SSE 380* index. Stock portfolios are formed based on the maximisation of the *FUN* of all stocks of tested indexes. The dashed thin top and bottom lines are the upper and lower bounds of the forecast confidence intervals. The dashed thick line represents the forecast values of the rolling return difference – in Figure a), and *SR* difference – in Figure b). The analysed historical period from May 2003 through March 2022, 227 months.

Source: Own research using ITSM ver. 7.1.

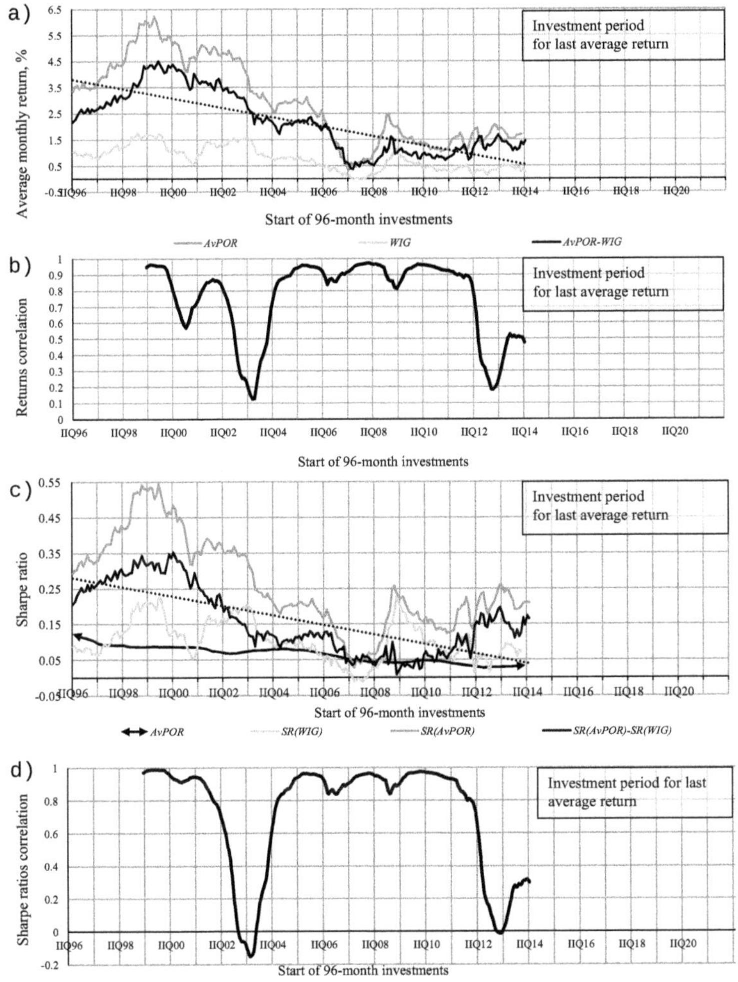

Figure 5.25 Rolling a) 96-month average returns, b) correlations between 96-month *WIG* formed portfolio and *WIG* index average returns, c) *SR* on 96 months: of *WIG* formed portfolio and *WIG* index, d) correlations between *SR* of *WIG* formed portfolio and *WIG* index.

Notes: *AvPOR* is a linearly weighted portfolio consisting of 15, 10, 7, and 5 stock portfolios formed on *WIG* index. Each point of the chart presents the examined portfolio characteristics [average return, correlations between *AvPOR* and *WIG* average returns, *SR*, correlations between *SR* of *AvPOR* and *SR* of *WIG* index, and ratio of 15

Figure 5.25 (Continued)

companies portfolio capitalisation (*CAP_P*) to the capitalisation of 50 companies with the maximum capitalisation of the index (*CAP_WIG*)] at the beginning of the 96-month investment period. *SR* of *AvPOR* is computed as the ratio of the average excess return on *AvPOR* over the average risk-free rate (*AvPOR-RF*) to the standard deviation of the excess return s(*AvPOR-RF*). *RF* is estimated based on U.S. 3-Month Treasury bills. *SR* of *WIG* is computed as the ratio of the average excess return on *WIG* over the average risk-free rate (*WIG-RF*) to the standard deviation of the excess return s(*WIG-RF*). Stock portfolios are formed based on the maximisation of the *FUN* of all stocks of *WIG*. The dotted line in Figure a) shows the trend line of changes in the differences between the average return on *AvPOR* and the average return on the *WIG* index. The dotted line in Figure c) shows the trend lines of changes in the differences between the *SR* of *AvPOR* (*SR(AvPOR)*) and the *SR* of the *WIG* index (*SR(WIG)*). The analysed historical period from May 1996 through March 2022, 311 months.

Source: Own research.

The time series curves of return and SR illustrate the variations over time for the formed portfolios and the entire index. The maximum average returns from 96 monthly investments in portfolios of 5, 7, 10, and 15 companies (with the highest FUN values) between 1996 and 2022 are 120.2%, 113.7%, 104.8%, and 88.0%, respectively, on a yearly basis. The minimum average returns for the same portfolios are 4.4%, 0.7%, 5.7%, and 6.2%, respectively, annually.

The maximum and minimum average returns for the average portfolio (formed from the 5, 7, 10, and 15 companies) between 1996 and 2022 are 106.7% and 4.2%, respectively. For the WIG index, the maximum and minimum average returns between 1996 and 2022 are 23.4% and -0.5%, respectively.

A careful examination of these figures reveals substantial differences in returns between the formed portfolios and the index between 1996 and 2006. However, these differences noticeably decrease from 2007 onwards, a trend also observable in the SR. The gap in average returns narrows from 3.6% to approximately 0.5%, while the SR difference decreases from 0.3 to around 0.05 (see Figures 5.25a and 5.25c). The largest fluctuations in the correlation coefficients between the returns of formed portfolios and the WIG index occurred between 2000–2005 and 2012–2014. The correlation decreased monotonically from approximately 0.9 in 2000 to 0.1 in 2003, then increased steadily to exceed 0.9 by 2006. From 2006 to 2012, the correlation remained near 1. It then decreased again between 2012 and 2013 to around 0.2, before rising to 0.5 in 2014. A similar pattern is seen in the correlation between the SRs of formed portfolios and the WIG index throughout the entire period (1996–2022) (see Figures 5.25b and 5.25d).

Changes in the ratio of the average capitalisation of the portfolio to that of the 50 companies with the highest capitalisation in the index show that the portfolio's relative capitalisation began increasing in 2004, peaking at 10%. A slight decline (around 2%) occurred after 2012. This shift may partly explain the reduced differences between the returns of the formed portfolios and the index post-2007.

Figure 5.26 illustrates rolling 60-month average returns (a), rolling correlations between the 60-month formed portfolios and WIG average returns (b), rolling SRs for the 60-month WIG average portfolios (formed from the 5, 7, 10, and 15 companies with the highest FUN values) and the WIG index (c), and rolling correlations between the SRs of WIG portfolios and the WIG index (d). The correlations are calculated using 36-month windows.
The time series curves of return and SR again reflect the variations over time for the formed portfolios and the entire index.

The maximum average returns from 60 monthly investments in portfolios of 5, 7, 10, and 15 companies (with the highest FUN values) between 1996 and 2022 are 189.7%, 174.0%, 159.3%, and 133.4%, respectively, annually. The minimum average returns for the same portfolios are -7.2%, -9.8%, -8.8%, and -9.5%, respectively.

The maximum and minimum average returns for the average portfolio (formed from the 5, 7, 10, and 15 companies) from 1996 to 2022 are 164.1% and -8.8%, respectively. For the WIG index, the maximum and minimum average returns between 1996 and 2022 are 40.1% and -7.0%, respectively.

As with the 96-month returns, a close inspection of these figures indicates significant differences between the returns of the formed portfolios and the WIG index between 1996 and 2006. These differences again diminish from 2007 onwards, with similar trends observed in the SR. The characteristic difference in average returns narrows from 3.6% to approximately 0.5%, and the SR difference decreases from 0.3 to about 0.05 (see Figures 5.26a and 5.26c).

The most significant changes in the correlation coefficients between the returns of the formed portfolios and the WIG index occurred between 2005–2007 and 2012–2017. The correlation dropped monotonically from around 0.9 in 2006 to 0.6 in 2007, then increased steadily, exceeding 0.9 in 2008. It remained close to 1 until 2011. From 2015 to 2016, the correlation fell again to about 0.1, before rising to 0.7 in 2017. A similar pattern is observed in the correlation between the SRs of the formed portfolios and the WIG index over the

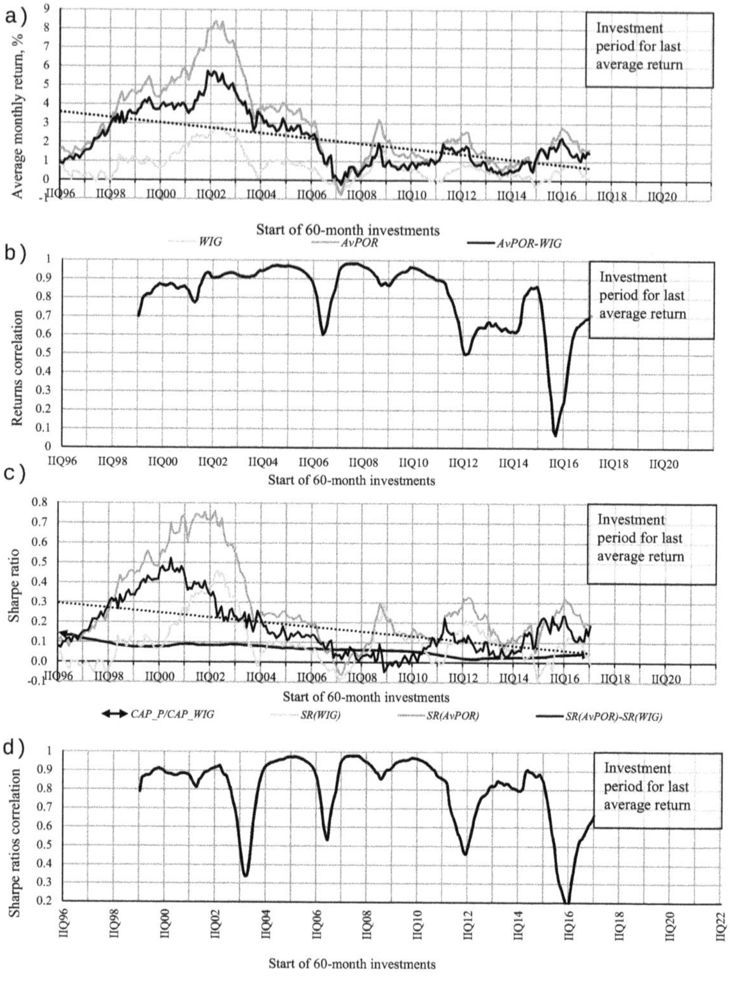

Figure 5.26 Rolling a) 60-month average returns, b) correlations between 60-month *WIG* formed portfolio and *WIG* index average returns, c) *SR* on 60 months: of *WIG* formed portfolio and *WIG* index, d) correlations between *SR* of *WIG* formed portfolio and *WIG* index.

Notes: *AvPOR* is a linearly weighted portfolio consisting of 15, 10, 7, and 5 stock portfolios formed on *WIG* index. Each point of the chart presents the examined portfolio characteristics [average return, correlations between *AvPOR* and *WIG* average returns, *SR*, correlations between *SR* of *AvPOR* and *SR* of *WIG* index, and ratio of 15 companies portfolio capitalisation (*CAP_P*) to the capitalisation of 50 companies with

Figure 5.26 (Continued)

the maximum capitalisation of the index (*CAP_WIG*)] at the beginning of the 96-month investment period. *SR* of *AvPOR* is computed as the ratio of the average excess return on *AvPOR* over the average risk-free rate (*AvPOR-RF*) to the standard deviation of the excess return s(*AvPOR-RF*). *RF* is estimated based on U.S. 3-Month Treasury bills. *SR* of *WIG* is computed as the ratio of the average excess return on *WIG* over the average risk-free rate (*WIG-RF*) to the standard deviation of the excess return s(*WIG-RF*). Stock portfolios are formed based on the maximisation of the *FUN* of all stocks of *WIG*. The dotted line in Figure a) shows the trend line of changes in the differences between the average return on *AvPOR* and the average return on the *WIG* index. The dotted line in Figure c) shows the trend lines of changes in the differences between the *SR* of *AvPOR* (*SR(AvPOR)*) and the *SR* of the *WIG* index (*SR(WIG)*). The analysed historical period from May 1996 through March 2022, 311 months.

Source: Own research.

1996–2022 period, with the coefficient fluctuating between 0.2 and 0.9 (see Figures 5.26b and 5.26d).

The ratio of the portfolio's average capitalisation to that of the 50 largest companies in the index decreased from 0.12 in 1996 to 2017. This trend may also partly explain the delayed reduction in differences between the returns of the formed portfolios and the index after 2007.

As before, we examine the time series of differences in returns (AvPOR-WIG) and SRs (SR(AvPOR)-SR(WIG)) between the formed portfolios and the index. Figure 5.27 presents SARIMA modelling to predict rolling differences between the 96-month average returns and SRs for the formed portfolios and the WIG index.

Table A.16 (provided in the Appendix) presents the key parameters of the applied SARIMA model.

As with the earlier models, the majority of the parameters are statistically significant. Forecasts derived from the Polish market data begin in Q2 2004. The SARIMA model indicates that the confidence interval for forecasted SR differences contains zero from Q3 2007 to Q2 2012 (see Figure 5.27b). Similarly, the confidence interval for forecasted return differences contains zero from Q3 2007 (see Figure 5.27a). Long-term forecasts show that both return and SR differences between the created portfolios and the WIG index tend towards zero, supporting the rejection of Conjectures 1 and 2.

Figure 5.28 presents the Holt–Winters method for predicting rolling differences between the average returns and SRs of the formed portfolios and the WIG index.

Table A.17 (provided in the Appendix) presents the key parameters of the Holt–Winters method. According to the Holt–Winters method, the predicted confidence intervals for SR differences contain zero

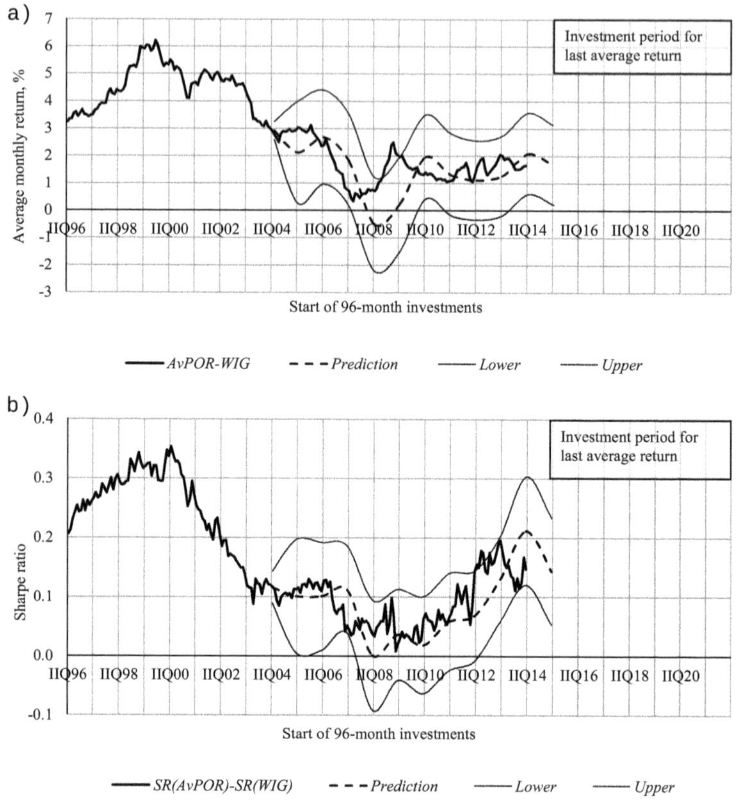

Figure 5.27 SARIMA modelling to predict rolling differences between a) average returns, b) *SR* on 96 months, corresponding to the formed portfolios and the values of *WIG* index.

Notes: Each point of the chart presents the examined portfolio characteristics (average return and *SR*) at the beginning of the 96-month investment period. *SR* is computed as the ratio of the average excess return from the examined portfolio over the average risk-free rate (*Rp-RF*) to the standard deviation of the excess return s(*Rp-RF*). *RF* is estimated based on U.S. 3-Month Treasury bills. *AvPOR* is a linearly weighted portfolio consisting of 15, 10, 7, and 5 stock portfolios formed on *WIG* index. Stock portfolios are formed based on the maximisation of the *FUN* of all stocks of *WIG*. The dashed thin top and bottom lines are the upper and lower bounds of the forecast confidence intervals. The dashed thick line represents the forecast values of the rolling return difference – in Figure a), and *SR* difference – in Figure b). The analysed historical period from May 1996 through March 2022, 311 months.

Source: Own research using R-Studio ver. 4.2.3.

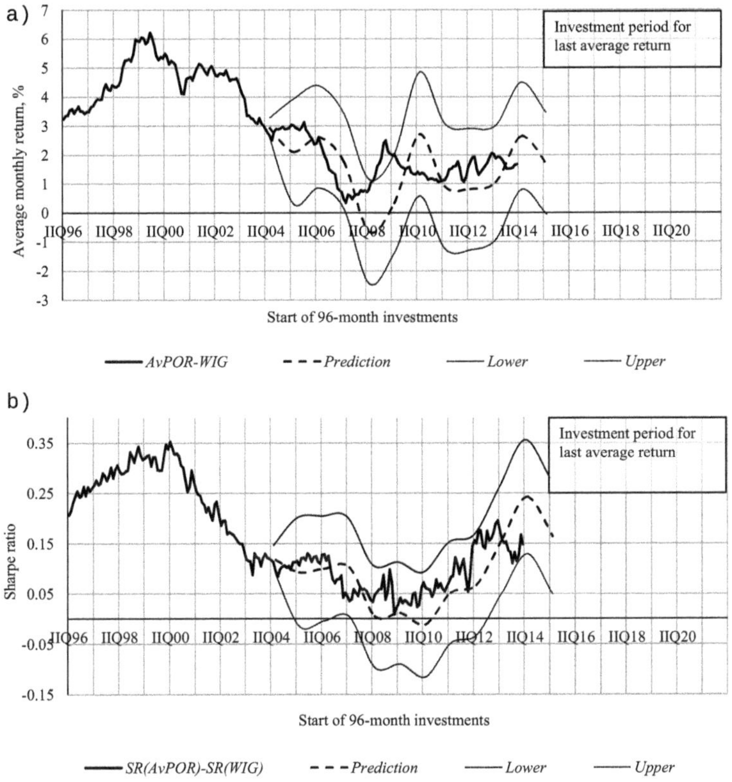

Figure 5.28 Holt–Winters method to predict rolling differences between a) average returns, b) *SR* on 96 months, corresponding to the formed portfolios and the values of *WIG* index.

Notes: Each point of the chart presents the examined portfolio characteristics (average return and *SR*) at the beginning of the 96-month investment period. *SR* is computed as the ratio of the average excess return from the examined portfolio over the average risk-free rate (*Rp-RF*) to the standard deviation of the excess return s(*Rp-RF*). *RF* is estimated based on U.S. 3-Month Treasury bills. *AvPOR* is a linearly weighted portfolio consisting of 15, 10, 7, and 5 stock portfolios formed on *WIG* index. Stock portfolios are formed based on the maximisation of the *FUN* of all stocks of tested indexes. The dashed thin top and bottom lines are the upper and lower bounds of the forecast confidence intervals. The dashed thick line represents the forecast values of the rolling return difference – in Figure a), and *SR* difference – in Figure b). The analysed historical period from May 1996 through March 2022, 311 months.

Source: Own research using ITSM ver. 7.1.

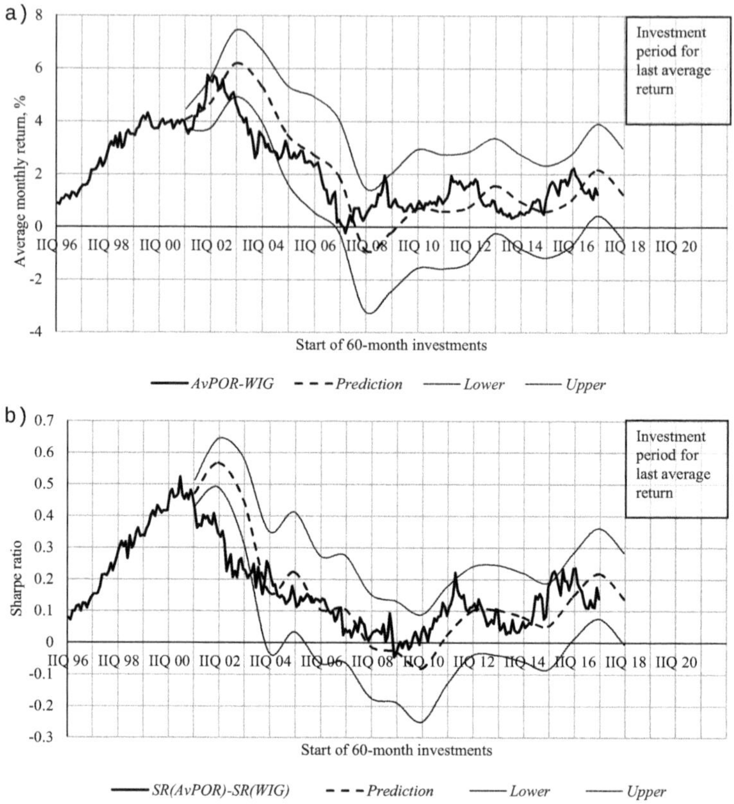

Figure 5.29 SARIMA and prediction of rolling differences between a) 60-month average returns, b) *SR* on 60 months, corresponding to the formed portfolios and the values of *WIG* index.

Notes: Each point of the chart presents the examined portfolio characteristics (average return and *SR*) at the beginning of the 60-month investment period. *SR* is computed as the ratio of the average excess return from the examined portfolio over the average risk-free rate (*Rp-RF*) to the standard deviation of the excess return s(*Rp-RF*). *RF* is estimated based on U.S. 3-Month Treasury bills. *AvPOR* is a linearly weighted portfolio consisting of 15, 10, 7, and 5 stock portfolios formed on *WIG* index. Stock portfolios are formed based on the maximisation of the *FUN* of all stocks of *WIG*. The dashed thin top and bottom lines are the upper and lower bounds of the forecast confidence intervals. The dashed thick line represents the forecast values of the rolling return difference – in Figure a), and *SR* difference – in Figure b). The analysed historical period from May 1996 through March 2022, 311 months.

Source: Own research using R-Studio ver. 4.2.3.

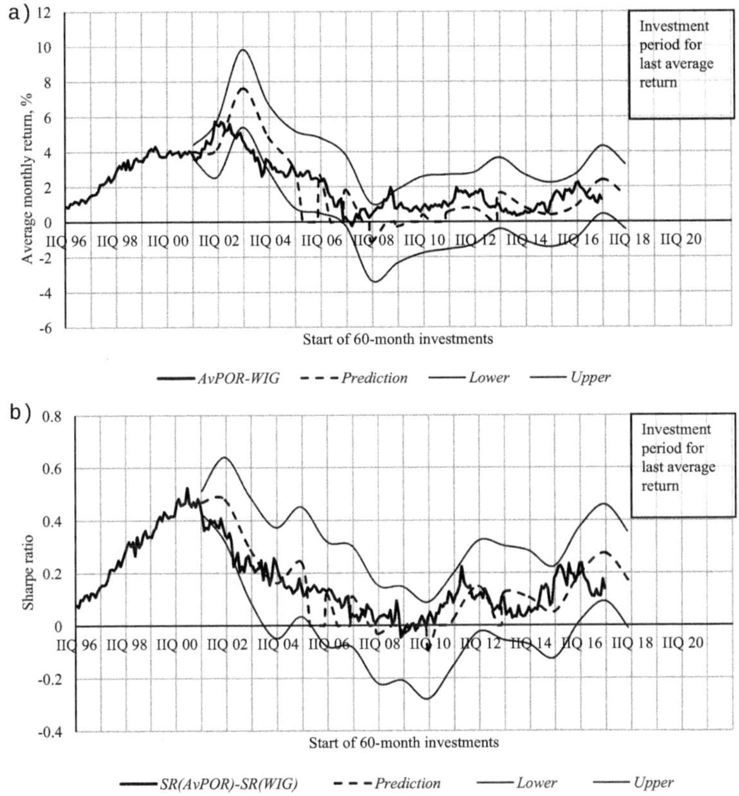

Figure 5.30 Holt–Winters method to predict rolling differences between a) 60-month average returns, b) SR on 96 months, corresponding to the formed portfolios and the values of WIG index.

Notes: Each point of the chart presents the examined portfolio characteristics (averaged return and *SR*) at the beginning of the 60-month investment period. *SR* is computed as the ratio of the average excess return from the examined portfolio over the average risk-free rate (*Rp-RF*) to the standard deviation of the excess return s(*Rp-RF*). *RF* is estimated based on U.S. 3-Month Treasury bills. *AvPOR* is a linearly weighted portfolio consisting of 15, 10, 7, and 5 stock portfolios formed on *WIG* index. Stock portfolios are formed based on the maximisation of the *FUN* of all stocks of tested indexes. The dashed thin top and bottom lines are the upper and lower bounds of the forecast confidence intervals. The dashed thick line represents the forecast values of the rolling return difference – in Figure a), and *SR* difference – in Figure b). The analysed historical period from May 1996 through March 2022, 311 months.

Source: Own research using ITSM ver. 7.1.

from Q4 2005 to Q2 2016 (see Figure 5.29b), a result also observed in the SARIMA model (see Figure 5.28b). The long-term forecasts suggest that both return and SR differences converge towards zero, indicating the rejection of Conjectures 1 and 2.

Figure 5.29 shows the SARIMA model predicting rolling differences between the 60-month average returns and SRs for the formed portfolios and the WIG index.

Table A.18 (provided in the Appendix) presents the key parameters of the SARIMA model.

Available data allow the calculation of confidence intervals for forecasts of differences in returns and SRs starting from Q2 2001. The SARIMA model shows that the confidence interval for forecasted SR differences contains zero from Q1 2005 to Q1 2016 (see Figure 5.29b), while the confidence interval for forecasted return differences contains zero from Q3 2006 (see Figure 5.29a). Long-term forecasts indicate that both return and SR differences between the portfolios and the WIG index converge towards zero, reinforcing the rejection of Conjectures 1 and 2.

Figure 5.30 illustrates the Holt–Winters method predicting rolling differences between the 60-month average returns and SRs for the formed portfolios and the WIG index.

Table A.19 (provided in the Appendix) presents the key parameters of the Holt–Winters method. The Holt–Winters method indicates that the predicted confidence intervals for SR differences contain zero from Q1 2006 to Q1 2016 (see Figure 5.30b), a result similar to the SARIMA model (see Figure 5.29b). The long-term forecasts suggest that both return and SR differences approach zero, confirming the rejection of Conjectures 1 and 2.

References

Chatfield, C. (1978). The Holt-Winters Forecasting Procedure. *Applied Statistics* 27 (3), 264–279.

Shumway, R.H., & Stoffer, D.S. (2011). *Time Series Analysis and Its Applications. With R Examples*. 3rd ed. New York: Springer.

6 Discussion

When analysing the research results in Section 5, the reader should note that the values of rolling returns represent 96-month or 60-month averages, assigned to the beginning of the first month. In other words, each abscissa in the figures reflects the average of values for the subsequent 96 or 60 months. Similarly, the market efficiency tests presented in Section 4 are based on average returns from 96- or 60-month investment periods. Consequently, inferences regarding market efficiency within the scope of this research pertain to investments spanning 96 or 60 months. This condition applies when a representative investor adopts long-term positions in an investment fund's assets.

To test the hypotheses outlined in Section 3.5, we compare the return and SR values of portfolios formed on FUN with those of benchmarked portfolios. Of particular interest are the differences in SR values (see Malkiel 2003, p. 60).

The methodological approach draws on the work of FF1995, who posited that future returns are driven by the structure of past financial results, rather than by HML and SMB factors. Thus, the Fama-French three-factor model (1993) could be modified to incorporate risk factors reflecting the structure of past financial outcomes. Such a modification, proposed by Urbański (2012), could offer an alternative application of the ICAPM. If a representative investor's portfolio is based on the structure of past financial results, returns on that portfolio should align with the ICAPM, suggesting that all investor portfolios yield similar returns per unit of risk, thereby forming a market portfolio. This would imply market efficiency.

These conclusions align with observed changes in the American, Polish, and, to some extent, Japanese markets post-2007. In each

DOI: 10.4324/9781003587330-6

case, the slope of the trend line depicting the differences between the returns of formed portfolios and the tested market indices is negative. This negative slope is evident for both 60-month and 96-month investment periods (see Figures 5.1 and 5.2 for the American market, Figures 5.13 and 5.14 for the Japanese market, and Figures 5.25 and 5.26 for the Polish market).

For the U.S. market, both 96-month and 60-month rolling investments show that the confidence intervals for predicted return and SR differences (using both the SARIMA and Holt-Winters models) contain zero from Q2 2007, across all tested periods.

For the Polish market with 60-month investments, the confidence intervals for the predicted return and SR differences also contain zero for all tested periods. Similarly, for 96-month investments on the Polish market, the confidence intervals for predicted return and SR differences contain zero for most periods.

For the Japanese market with 60-month investments, the confidence intervals for forecasted SR differences using the Holt–Winters method contain zero from Q1 2010. When using the SARIMA model, zero values for forecasted SR differences appear at the lower limit of the confidence intervals.

Changes in returns on the Chinese market are more complex. Early in the first decade of the 21st century, there were signs of market efficiency. However, due to limited data availability, it was not possible to apply the SARIMA and Holt–Winters models to forecast differences in returns and SR during this period. In the second decade, the changes in returns on the formed portfolios and the SSE 380 index diverged from those observed in other markets. The slope of the trend line showing the differences between the portfolio returns and the index became positive.

In contrast, the BE 500 index exhibited different patterns of return and SR changes compared to the other markets. Throughout the testing period, differences between the returns and SRs of the formed portfolios and the index changed slowly. However, the confidence intervals for the forecasts of return and SR differences (modelled using the SARIMA and Holt–Winters methods) consistently contained zero. For 96-month investments, the confidence intervals included zero from Q3 2010. For 60-month investments, this occurred from Q2 2006.

To confirm the influence of a representative investor on these market changes, we examine shifts in the investor structure during the tested periods. Figures 6.1 to 6.5 illustrate changes in the investor structure, share distribution, and stock capitalisation across the American, European, Japanese, Chinese, and Polish markets in the first two decades of the 21st century. The share of each investor group is calculated as the ratio of the stock capitalisation held by that group to the total stock capitalisation.

An increase in the share of institutional investors is observed in both the U.S. and European markets, starting in 2007 and 2005, respectively. On the U.S. market, institutional investors' share increased by 37% in 2007–2008 and by 35% in 2009–2021. On the European market, the increase was 110% in 2005–2009 and 42% in 2009–2021. This rise is accompanied by a delayed decline in the stock capitalisation of this group during 2007–2008, falling by 39% in the United States and 53% in Europe. However, from 2009 to 2021, capitalisation increased substantially: by 760% on the U.S. market and 235% on the European market. Over the same period, the share and capitalisation structure of corporate and large individual investors remained largely unchanged, though a slight increase in the capitalisation of stocks held by the 'Corporation' group was noted on the European market after 2009. The shares of these investors remain several times lower than those of institutional investors.

The share of small individual investors consistently declined over the period. In the United States, the greatest decline occurred in 2007–2008, with a reduction of 24%, followed by 35% in 2009–2021. On the European market, the respective declines were 18% and 28%. This decline in shares was mirrored by a decrease in capitalisation on the U.S. market by 64% from 2007 to 2009, followed by a 318% increase from 2009 to 2021. However, this growth was several times lower than the 760% increase in institutional investors' capitalisation (see Figure 6.1b). On the European market, small investors' capitalisation declined by approximately 72% in 2007–2009, then increased by 78% in 2009–2021 (see Figure 6.2b).

The changes in the share of institutional and small individual investors indicate that, from 2008 to 2009 onward, the representative investor in the U.S. market is an institutional investor. If the perspective of an institutional investor, such as an investment fund, is considered long-term, investment decisions are likely based on past long-term financial performance (FF1995). This investor behaviour explains the observed changes in returns on the U.S. stock market (see Section 5.1, Figures 5.1–5.6).

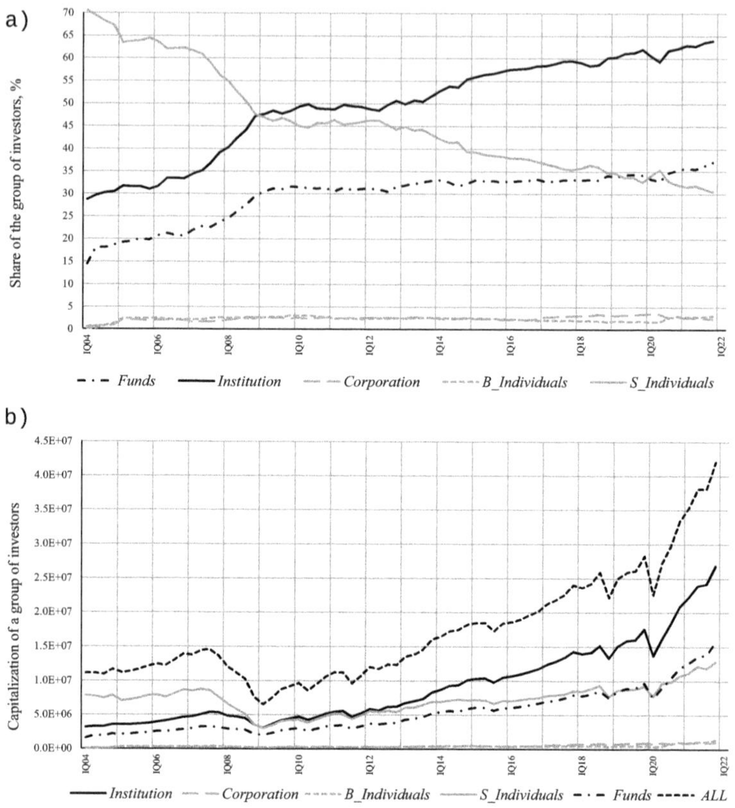

Figure 6.1 The structure of individual investor groups investing in *S&P 500* index companies; a) share of the group of investors at the end of the quarter periods; b) capitalisation of the investor groups.

Notes: The share of the examined group of investors is calculated as the ratio of the capitalisation of stocks held by a given group to the capitalisation of all groups. 'Institution' includes public and private investment firms. 'Funds' includes private and public funds. The Funds are included in the Institution group. 'Corporation' includes all company types excluding the public and private investment firms. 'B_Individuals' includes individuals listed by the stock exchange as shareholders. 'S_Individuals' incudes small individuals investors. 'ALL' includes all firms of *S&P 500* index.

Source: Own elaboration using the EquityRT database.

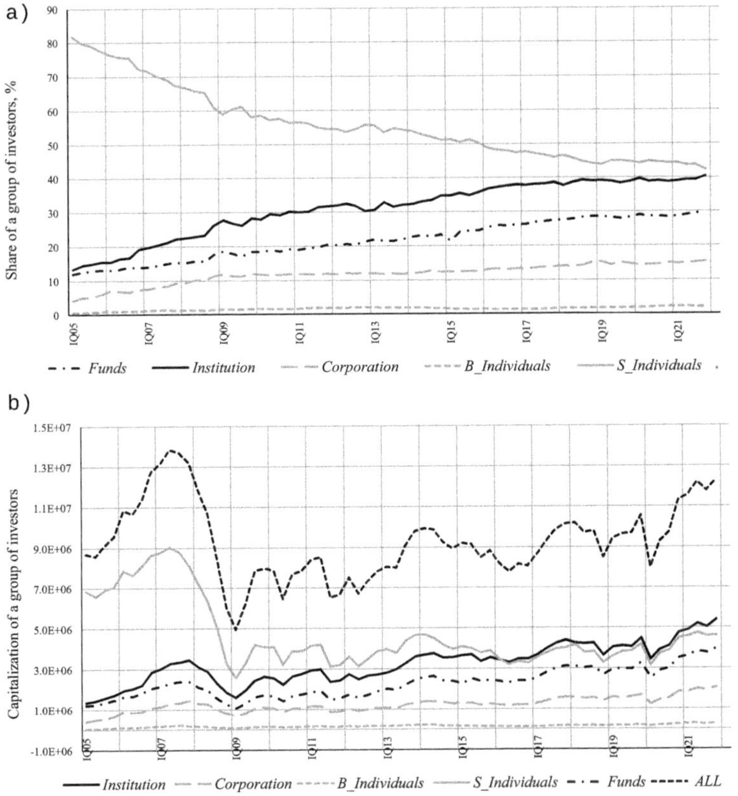

Figure 6.2 The structure of individual investor groups investing in *BE 500* index companies; a) share of the group of investors at the end of the quarter periods; b) capitalisation of the investor groups.

Notes: The share of the examined group of investors is calculated as the ratio of the capitalisation of stocks held by a given group to the capitalisation of all groups. 'Institution' includes public and private investment firms. 'Funds' includes private and public funds. The Funds are included in the Institution group. 'Corporation' includes all company types excluding the public and private investment firms. 'B_Individuals' includes individuals listed by the stock exchange as shareholders. 'S_Individuals' incudes small individuals investors. 'ALL' includes all firms of *BE 500* index.

Source: Own elaboration using the EquityRT database.

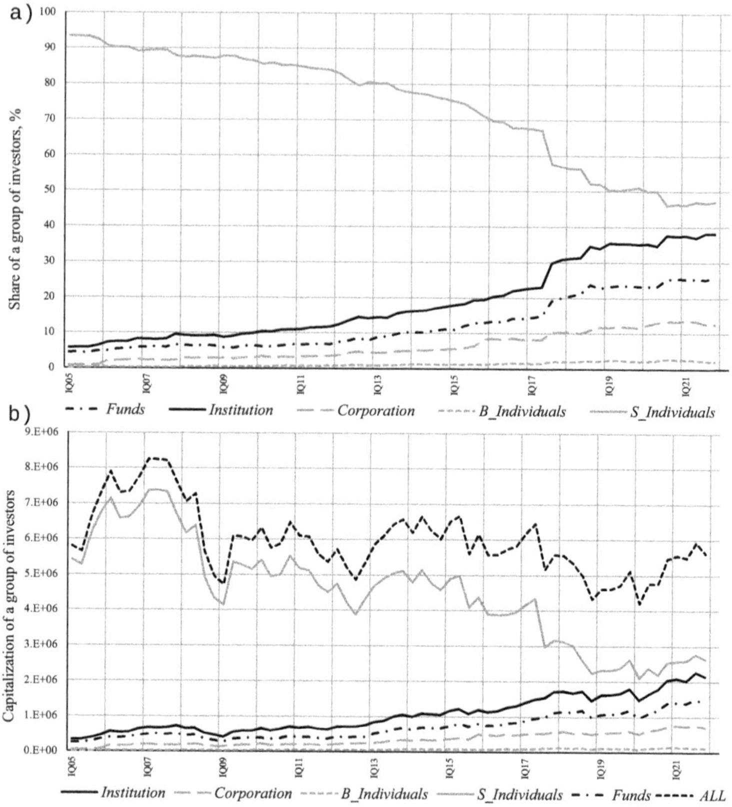

Figure 6.3 The structure of individual investor groups investing in *TOPIX 500* index companies; a) share of the group of investors at the end of the quarter periods; b) capitalisation of the investor groups.

Notes: The share of the examined group of investors is calculated as the ratio of the capitalisation of stocks held by a given group to the capitalisation of all groups. 'Institution' includes public and private investment firms. 'Funds' includes private and public funds. The Funds are included in the Institution group. 'Corporation' includes all company types excluding the public and private investment firms. 'B_Individuals' includes individuals listed by the stock exchange as shareholders. 'S_Individuals' incudes small individuals investors. 'ALL' includes all firms of *TOPIX 500* index.

Source: Own elaboration using the EquityRT database.

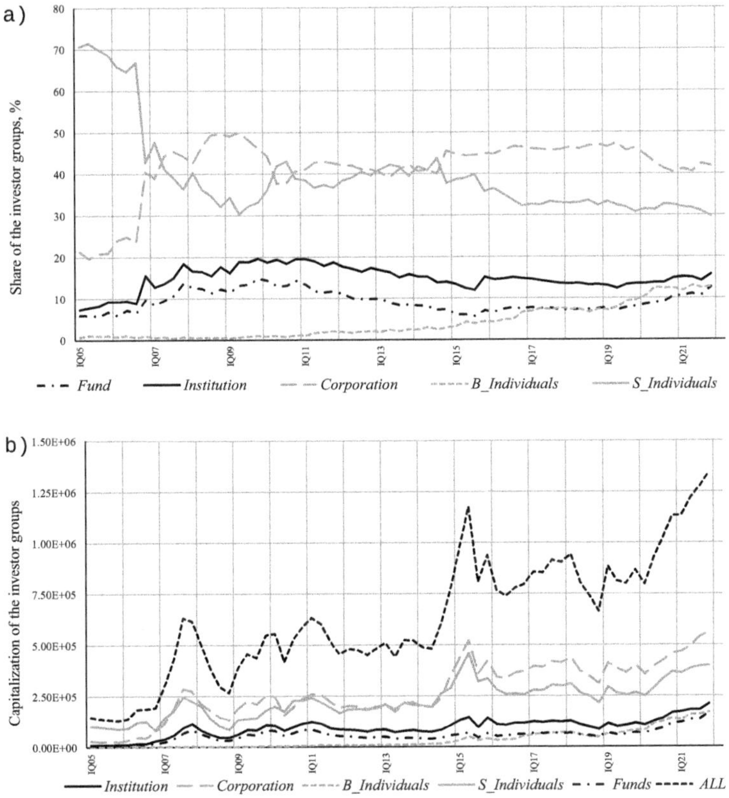

Figure 6.4 The structure of individual investor groups investing in *SSE 380* index companies; a) share of the group of investors at the end of the quarter periods; b) capitalisation of the investor groups.

Notes: The share of the examined group of investors is calculated as the ratio of the capitalisation of stocks held by a given group to the capitalisation of all groups. 'Institution' includes public and private investment firms. Funds includes private and public funds. 'Corporation' includes all company types excluding the public and private investment firms. 'B_Individuals' includes individuals listed by the stock exchange as shareholders. 'S_Individuals' incudes small individuals investors. 'ALL' includes all firms of *SSE 380* index.

Source: Own elaboration using the EquityRT database.

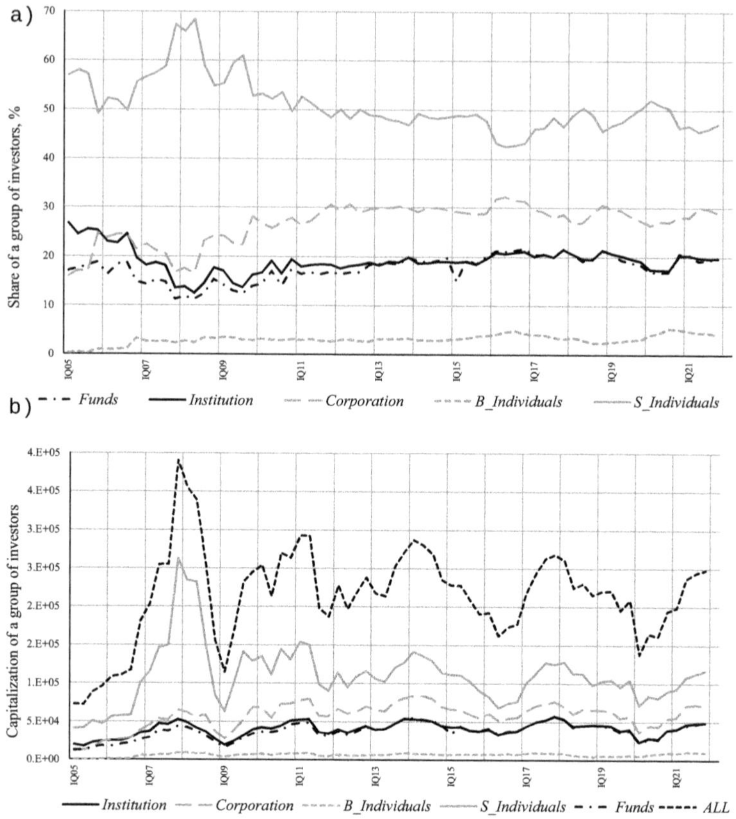

Figure 6.5 The structure of individual investor groups investing in *WIG* index companies; a) share of the group of investors at the end of the quarter periods; b) capitalisation of the investor groups.

Notes: The share of the examined group of investors is calculated as the ratio of the capitalisation of stocks held by a given group to the capitalisation of all groups. 'Institution' includes public and private investment firms. Funds includes private and public funds. 'Corporation' includes all company types excluding the public and private investment firms. 'B_Individuals' includes individuals listed by the stock exchange as shareholders. 'S_Individuals' incudes small individuals investors. 'ALL' includes all firms of *WIG* index.

Source: Own elaboration using the EquityRT database.

In the case of the European market, the decline in small individual investors' shares began in 2005, with the largest decreases occurring in 2005–2009. Conversely, institutional investors' shares increased steadily from 2005, with the largest increases observed in 2005–2009. These shifts suggest that, by the second decade of the 21st century, the institutional investor has taken over the role of the representative investor, explaining the changes in returns on the European market (see Section 5.2, Figures 5.7–5.12).

The changes in shares and capitalisation in the Japanese market mirror those in the European market. Between 2005 and 2021, the share of small individual investors fell by around 50%, compared to 48% in the European market. Similarly, institutional investors' shares grew by approximately 576% in Japan, compared to 200% in Europe. Capitalisation of small investors in Japan decreased by about 51%, whereas in Europe it declined by 28%. For institutional investors, capitalisation increased by 557% in Japan and 294% in Europe over the same period. The dynamics of the Japanese market, however, were slower in the first decade of the 21st century and faster in the second decade (see Figures 6.2a, 6.2b, and 6.3a, 6.3b). These changes suggest that the institutional investor has become the representative investor in Japan, similar to Europe but with greater momentum in the second decade. This is likely to result in wider forecasted confidence intervals for differences in average return and SR values on the European market (see Section 5.2, Figures 5.9a, 5.9b–5.12a, 5.12b and 5.15a, 5.15b–5.18a, 5.18b). The negative slopes in the trend lines of return and SR differences on the Japanese market (see Figures 5.13a, 5.13c, and 5.14a, 5.14c) contrast with the positive slopes observed in the European market (see Figures 5.7a, 5.7c, and 5.8a, 5.8c). These trends reflect the influence of institutional investors' decisions on returns in Japan during the second decade of the 21st century (see Section 5.3, Figures 5.13–5.18).

In the Chinese market, until 2007, small individual investors were the representative investors, with decisions based on the principles outlined by FF1995, possibly preceding the decisions of U.S. investors. From 2007 onwards, corporate investors began to dominate, while institutional investors remained less significant. Political regulations, which are beyond the scope of this analysis, may explain these shifts. Consequently, the changes in returns on the Chinese market before 2007–2008 (illustrated in Figures 5.19a, 5.19c, and 5.20a, 5.20c) could be attributed to small individual investors. However, due to the limited data for 2007–2008, quantitative verification using models such as SARIMA or Holt–Winters is not possible. From 2009 to 2022, the shares and capitalisation of corporate investors and small individual investors stabilised, with higher values compared to institutional investors. Furthermore, the decreasing ratio of portfolio capitalisation to the capitalisation of firms in the SSE 380 index (CAP_P/CAP_SSE) from 0.13 in 2003 to approximately 0.03 in 2007 indicates that, in this period, the returns of portfolios were primarily influenced by large-cap companies. This downward trend in the CAP_P/CAP_SSE ratio aligns with the observed trends in returns and SRs of index and portfolio returns.

Changes in the shares and market capitalisation of stocks within the WIG index, particularly those of small individual investors, in comparison to other investor groups, demonstrate that small individual investors remain representative throughout the period analysed. The largest discrepancies between the shares and capitalisation of small individual investors and those from other groups occurred between 2007 and 2009, but these differences diminished in subsequent years. Nevertheless, the transactions of small individual investors in the Polish market are increasingly influenced by foreign individual investors, who primarily focus on the U.S. market as the global leader. The proportion of foreign investors in trading on the Warsaw Stock Exchange's main market rose from 36% in 2009 to 64% in 2022 (www.gpw.pl/analizy). This behaviour in the Polish market may help explain the observed similarities in returns and SRs relative to movements in the U.S. market (see Figures 5.25–5.30).

The changes observed since 2007 in the United States, Polish, and EU markets can also be attributed to the growing significance of Exchange-Traded Funds (ETFs). ETF market capitalisation has steadily increased, surpassing USD 10 trillion in 2023 (Shih et al. 2024). The three largest ETFs globally, which track the S&P 500 index we examined, each has a capitalisation exceeding USD 500 billion. As of October 25, 2024, the market capitalisation of the SPDR S&P 500 ETF Trust was USD 599.98 billion; iShares Core S&P 500 ETF, USD 544.33 billion; and Vanguard S&P 500 ETF, USD 543.06 billion. In general, ETFs reflect the U.S. market's dominance. In Poland, however, the ETF market is still relatively small, with only 13 ETFs available on the Warsaw Stock Exchange, of which five track Polish indices.

In 2022, global investments in mutual funds, ETFs, and institutional funds totalled USD 60.1 trillion, with USD 28.6 trillion in the United States, USD 19.1 trillion in Europe, USD 9.1 trillion in the Asia-Pacific region, and USD 3.4 trillion across other regions. Over 57% of these funds were allocated to equity or balanced/mixed types. U.S.-based investment companies played a dominant role, with investments in the U.S. market totalling USD 22.1 trillion (77%), Europe USD 6.5 trillion (34%), Asia-Pacific USD 252 billion (2.8%), and other regions USD 73 billion (2.2%) (Investment Company Institute 2023). While the dominance of U.S. investors in their domestic funds is unsurprising, the significant share in the European market, surpassing one-third, is noteworthy. This may partially explain the observed similarities in the results for the U.S. and Polish markets.

From the perspective of U.S. market results, the share of actively managed domestic equity mutual funds and ETFs, as well as index-based domestic equity mutual funds and ETFs, in total market capitalisation has steadily increased from 2012 to 2019, remaining at or above 30% (32% in 2022) from 2019 to 2022 (Investment Company Institute 2023). Converse et al. (2023) suggest that the greater use of ETFs as a conduit for capital flows into emerging markets has heightened these economies' exposure to the global financial cycle. Furthermore, they argue that the growing popularity of passively managed, benchmarked instruments contributes to market co-movement and synchronisation of capital flows, often at the expense of local fundamentals. This insight may offer an explanation for the similarities in results between the U.S. and Polish markets.

Prior to the global financial crisis of 2007, the U.S. market exhibited inefficiency, which allowed for above-average profits. This inefficiency may have been linked to two major market bubbles: the internet bubble of the early 2000s and the housing bubble of 2007. The market frenzy for technology stocks and later for real estate, particularly those financed by financial institutions, may have led to a departure from valuations based on fundamental data. It should also be noted that the inefficiency could be attributed to the poor quality and low reliability of published data, compounded by insufficient regulatory oversight. Following the crisis, regulatory changes, such as the Dodd-Frank Wall Street Reform and Consumer Protection Act and the Emergency Economic Stabilisation Act, likely contributed to increased market efficiency. Gurgul et al. (2021) showed that for the Austrian market, the impact of unexpected U.S. news was strongest during the global financial crisis of 2007–2009, while the strength of stock price changes implied by announcements decreased after that period.

The importance of sustainable development is reflected in the modest yet growing share of funds adhering to the ESG criteria, which increased from 5% in 2019 to 7.7% in 2022 (Investment Company Institute 2023).

Changes in corporate reporting, particularly in social and environmental areas, also have significant implications for market efficiency in Europe, the United States, and Poland. The extension of reporting requirements has enhanced the transparency of financial activities, especially in the European Union, where several legal regulations, such as Directive 2013/34/EU, Regulation (EU) 575/2013, Directive 2014/95/EU, and others, have been introduced.

Additionally, research supports the effectiveness of markets driven by ESG-focused companies (e.g., Goel and Sahay 2023).

The SARS-CoV-2 pandemic and accompanying restrictions significantly impacted financial markets, though the effects varied across regions. According to Spelta et al. (2023), 'the market response to the SARS-CoV-2 news generates volatility rates that decay over time as a power law, here interpreted as market inefficiency in processing the flow of information'. These authors also observed that countries previously affected by the pandemic experienced shocks just before announcements, which were subsequently absorbed quickly.

The inefficiency of the Chinese market during the COVID-19 period is also supported by the research of Ameer et al. (2023), who highlight its volatile structure. However, they also note that the measures taken by Chinese authorities to stimulate the economy and financial markets during the pandemic led to significant improvements in market efficiency post-pandemic. Our own study further corroborates this, showing statistical significance for the period following the end of the pandemic.

The efficiency of the U.S. market can be partly attributed to the growing role of automation and algorithmic trading. As Yuferova (2024) points out, 'an exogenous shock to algorithmic trading leads to an overall improvement in market efficiency via faster incorporation of information embedded in the market and limit order flows alike'. The boom in algorithmic trading in the United States began at the close of the first decade of the 21st century, with algorithmic trading accounting for 73% of U.S. securities markets in 2009 (McGowan

2010), and the volume of algorithmic trading increasing by 164% from 2005 to 2009 (Duhigg 2009). Moreover, Chaboud et al. (2009) found a higher correlation between algorithmic and non-algorithmic transactions, indicating reduced strategy differentiation. Hendershott and Riordan (2009) also observed that algorithmic trading contributed to enhanced market efficiency.

References

Ameer, S., Nor, S.M., Ali, S., & Zawawi, N.H.M. (2023). The Impact of COVID-19 on BRICS and MSCI Emerging Markets Efficiency: Evidence from MF-DFA. *Fractal and Fractional* 7 (519), 1–23.

Chaboud, A., Chiquoine, B., Hjalmarsson, E., & Vega, C. (2009). Rise of the Machines: Algorithmic Trading in the Foreign Exchange Market. Board of Governors of the Federal Reserve System. *International Finance Discussion Papers* 980, 1–44.

Converse, N., Levy-Yeyati, E., & Williams, T. (2023). How ETFs Amplify the Global Financial Cycle in Emerging Markets. *Review of Financial Studies* 36 (9), 3423–3462.

Duhigg, C. (2009). Stock Traders Find Speed Pays, in Milliseconds. *New York Times*, July 23.

Fama, E.F., & French, K.R. (1993). Common Risk Factors in the Returns on Stocks and Bonds. *Journal of Financial Economics* 33, 3–56.

Fama, E.F., & French, K.R. (1995). Size and Book-to-Market Factors in Earnings and Returns. *Journal of Finance* 50 (1), 131–155.

Goel, A., & Sahay, N. (2023). Investigating the Market Efficiency of Socially Responsible Indices: Evidence from India. *International Journal of Finance, Economics and Business* 2 (4), 301–312.

Gurgul, H., Mittere, C., & Wójtowicz, T. (2021). The Impact of US Macroeconomic News on the Prices of Single Stocks on the Vienna Stock Exchange. *Central European Journal of Economic Modelling and Econometrics* 13, 287–329.

Hendershott, T., & Riordan, R. (2009). *Algorithmic Trading and Information.* Working Papers 09-08, NET Institute.

Investment Company Institute (2023). *Investment Company Fact Book. A Review of Trends and Activities in the Investment Company Industry.* www.ici.org/system/files/2023-05/2023-factbook.pdf (Accessed March 25, 2025)

Malkiel, B.G. (2003). The Efficient Market Hypothesis and Its Critics. *Journal of Economic Perspective* 17 (1), 59–82.

McGowan, M.J. (2010). The Rise of Computerized High Frequency Trading: Use and Controversy. *Duke Law & Technology Review* 016.

Shih, K.-H., Wang, Y.-H., Kao, I.-C., & Lai, F.-M. (2024). Forecasting ETF Performance: A Comparative Study of Deep Learning Models and the Fama-French Three-Factor Model. *Mathematics* 12, 3158.

Spelta, A., Pecora, N., Flori, A., & Giudici, P. (2023). The Impact of the SARS-CoV-2 Pandemic on Financial Markets: A Seismologic Approach. *Annals of Operations Research* 330 (1/2), 639–664.

Urbański, S. (2012). Multifactor Explanations of Returns on the Warsaw Stock Exchange in Light of the ICAPM. *Economic Systems* 36 (4), 552–570.

Yuferova, D. (2024). Algorithmic Trading and Market Efficiency Around the Introduction of the NYSE Hybrid Market. *Journal of Financial Markets* 69, 100909.

7 Conclusions

This study investigates whether the average stock returns of the representative investor across the United States, European, Japanese, Chinese, and Polish markets align with Merton's ICAPM theory and whether these markets exhibit efficiency. We assess market efficiency by examining whether the test portfolios generate 96- and 60-month returns and risks that are not significantly different from those of stock indices. The portfolios are constructed based on Fama and French's (1995) premise that future returns are shaped by the structure of past long-term financial outcomes. The following conclusions emerge from our analysis:

1. The research on the U.S. market indicates that the average 96- and 60-month returns and SR values of the formed portfolios are not significantly different from those of the S&P 500 index during 2007–2022. This suggests that the U.S. stock market was efficient during this period. The primary factor for these outcomes appears to be the dominance of investment funds, which can be considered representative investors making decisions aligned with ICAPM guidelines. This finding has significant implications for investment fund managers.
2. The research on the European market reveals no significant differences between the average returns and SR values of the formed portfolios and the BE 500 index during 2010–2022. This supports the conclusion that the European stock market was efficient in this period. Similar to the U.S. market, the dominant role of investment funds in the second decade of the 21st century likely influenced these results.

DOI: 10.4324/9781003587330-7

3. The study of the Japanese market shows substantial differences between the average returns and SR values of the formed portfolios and the TOPIX 500 index over the 2004–2022 period. However, by the end of the study period, these differences diminish: for 96-month investments, the disparity in average monthly returns reduces from 1% to 0.05%, and the SR from 0.15 to 0.01; for 60-month investments, the differences in average returns decrease from 1.2% to 0.0%, and the SR from 0.15 to 0.0. Time series statistical analysis suggests that the Japanese stock market was inefficient during 2004–2022. This inefficiency may stem from the increasing influence of small individual investors, compared to institutional investors, in the latter years of the second decade.
4. The research on the Chinese market reveals two distinct periods. Prior to 2007, the returns and SR values of the formed portfolios were closely aligned with those of the SSE 380 index, reflecting the role of small individual investors whose decisions led to a return structure similar to that observed in the U.S. market. From 2007 onwards, however, the differences between the returns of the formed portfolios and the SSE 380 index grew. This shift reflects a change in the representative investor from small individual investors to corporate investors, with the role of institutional investors becoming negligible. Time series statistical tests show that the Chinese stock market was inefficient from 2005 to 2022.
5. The research on the Polish market indicates that similar to the U.S. market, the average returns and SR values of the formed portfolios are not significantly different from those of the WIG index in 2007–2022. This suggests that the Polish stock market was efficient during this period. Despite the representative investor being a small individual investor, the significant influence of individual foreign investors – primarily focused on the U.S. market – likely explains these results.

Reference

Fama, E.F., & French, K.R. (1995). Size and Book-to-Market Factors in Earnings and Returns. *Journal of Finance* 50 (1), 131–155.

8 Research limitations and future research directions

The limitations of the present research are as follows:

A. The study focused only on companies included in the major indices of the United States, European, Japanese, Chinese, and Polish markets (i.e., S&P 500, BE 500, TOPIX 500, SSE 380, and WIG). This limitation was due to the unavailability of the required financial data for other companies from these markets in the Bloomberg database.
B. Research on additional global markets would significantly extend the scope of this study.
C. The study utilised different time series based on the availability of financial data in the Bloomberg database.
D. The analysis of past financial performance used a specified form of the FUN functional, which is a sufficient (but not necessary) condition for forecasting future returns. Other forms of the FUN function may offer a better approximation of the observed results.
E. The method for portfolio simulation – using linearly weighted portfolios of 5, 7, 10, and 15 companies – was chosen arbitrarily.
F. The hypothetical investment periods of the representative investor (60 and 96 months) were also assumed arbitrarily.
G. Alternative methods for testing the validity of the return description under ICAPM could be explored, including Wald tests, Gibbons et al.'s (1989) test, as well as correct pricing tests by Shanken (1985) and Roll (1985). These statistics could be examined using rolling time windows across the historical periods considered.

DOI: 10.4324/9781003587330-8

References

Gibbons, M.R., Ross, S.A., & Shanken, J. (1989). A Test of the Efficiency of a Given Portfolio. *Econometrica* 57 (5), 1121–1152.

Roll, R. (1985). A Note on the Geometry of Shanken CSR T^2 Test for Mean/Variance Efficiency. *Journal of Financial Economics* 14, 349–357.

Shanken, J. (1985). Multivariate Tests of the Zero-Beta CAPM. *Journal of Financial Economics* 14 (3), 327–348.

Appendix

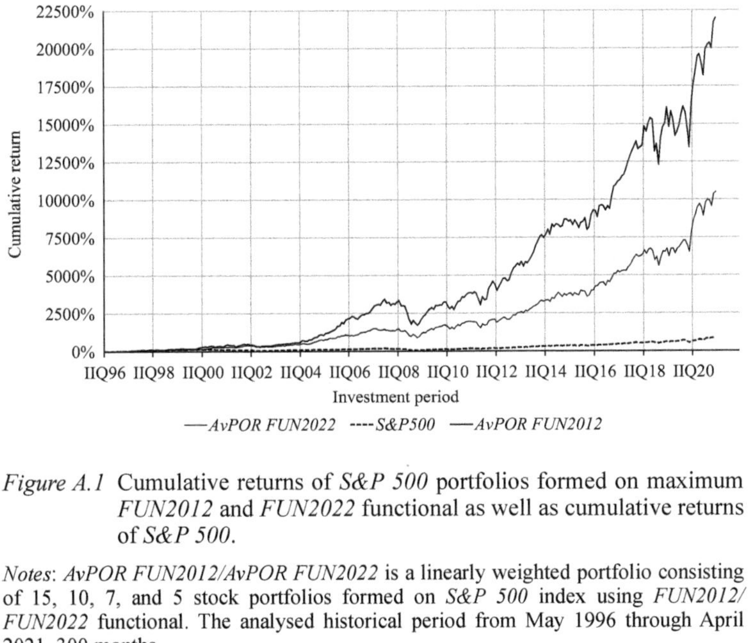

Figure A.1 Cumulative returns of *S&P 500* portfolios formed on maximum *FUN2012* and *FUN2022* functional as well as cumulative returns of *S&P 500*.

Notes: *AvPOR FUN2012/AvPOR FUN2022* is a linearly weighted portfolio consisting of 15, 10, 7, and 5 stock portfolios formed on *S&P 500* index using *FUN2012/FUN2022* functional. The analysed historical period from May 1996 through April 2021, 300 months.

Source: Own research.

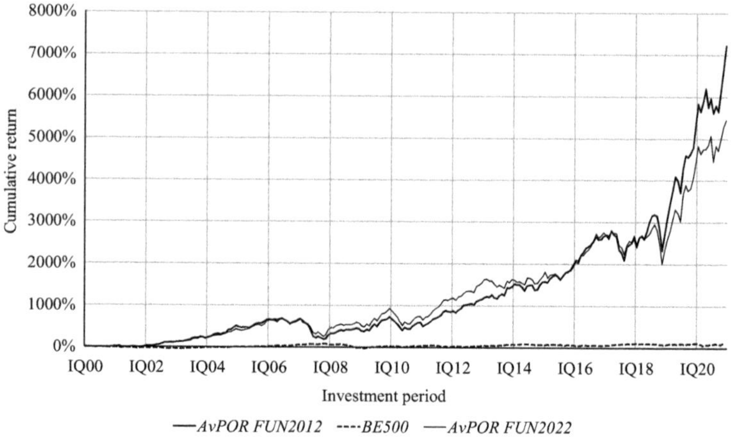

Figure A.2 Cumulative returns of *BE 500* portfolios formed on maximum *FUN2012* and *FUN2022* functions as well as cumulative returns of *BE 500*.

Notes: *AvPOR FUN2012/AvPOR FUN2022* is a linearly weighted portfolio consisting of 15, 10, 7, and 5 stock portfolios formed on *BE 500* index using *FUN2012/FUN2022* functional. The analysed historical period from May 2001 through April 2022, 252 months.

Source: Own research.

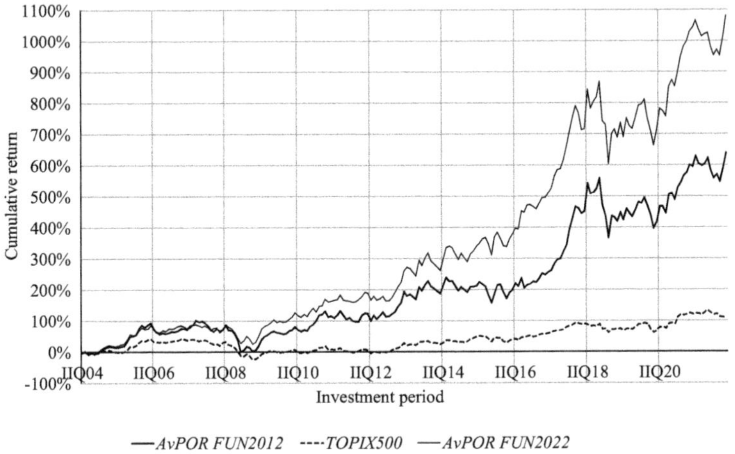

Figure A.3 Cumulative returns of *TOPIX 500* portfolios formed on maximum *FUN2012* and *FUN2022* functions as well as cumulative returns of *TOPIX 500*.

Notes: *AvPOR FUN2012/AvPOR FUN2022* is a linearly weighted portfolio consisting of 15, 10, 7, and 5 stock portfolios formed on *TOPIX 500* index using *FUN2012/ FUN2022* functional. The analysed historical period from May 2004 through April 2022, 216 months.

Source: Own research.

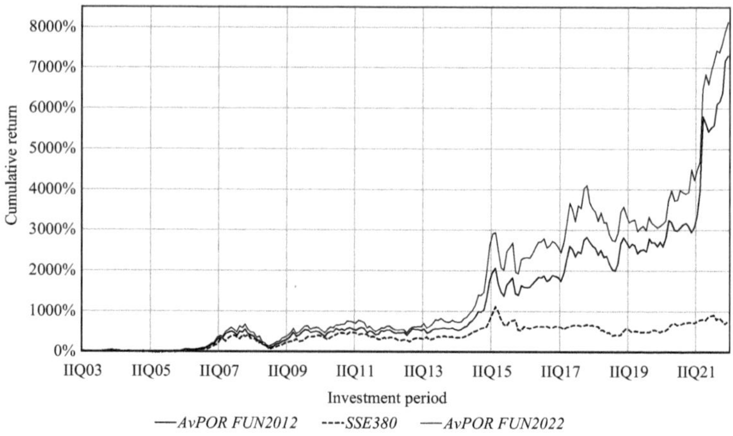

Figure A.4 Cumulative returns of *SSE 380* portfolios formed on maximum *FUN2012* and *FUN2022* functions as well as cumulative returns of *SSE 380*.

Notes: *AvPOR FUN2012/AvPOR FUN2022* is a linearly weighted portfolio consisting of 15, 10, 7, and 5 stock portfolios formed on *SSE 380* index using *FUN2012/FUN2022* functional. The analysed historical period from May 2003 through April 2022, 228 months.

Source: Own research.

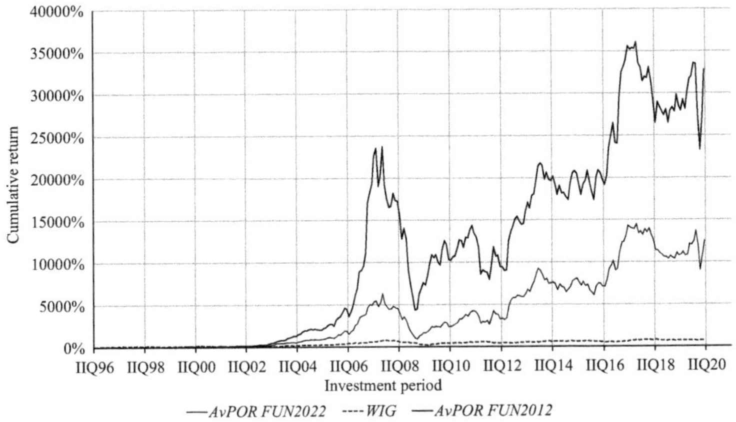

Figure A.5 Cumulative returns of *WIG* portfolios formed on maximum *FUN2012* and *FUN2022* functions as well as cumulative returns of *WIG*.

Notes: *AvPOR FUN2012*/*AvPOR FUN2022* is a linearly weighted portfolio consisting of 15, 10, 7, and 5 stock portfolios formed on *WIG* index using *FUN2012*/*FUN2022* functional. The analysed historical period from May 1996 through April 2020, 288 months.

Source: Own research.

Table A.1 Average annual effective return for portfolios formed on FUN and for tested indexes

	Average portfolios formed on tested indexes				
	S&P 500	*BE 500*	*TOPIX 500*	*SSE 380*	*WIG*
Period	1996-2021	2001-2022	2004-2022	2003-2022	1996-2020
Month No	300	252	216	228	288
AvPOR FUN2012	24.09%	22.68%	11.81%	25.42%	27.30%
AvPOR FUN2022	20.50%	21.08%	14.77%	26.13%	22.33%
Δ(FUN2012/FUN2022)	1.18	1.08	0.80	0.97	1.22
Index	9.75%	3.50%	4.21%	12.42%	8.83%
Δ(FUN2012/Index)	2.47	6.48	2.81	2.05	3.09
Δ(FUN2022/Index)	2.10	6.02	3.51	2.10	2.53

Notes: *AvPOR FUN2012/AvPOR FUN2022* is a linearly weighted portfolio consisting of 15, 10, 7 and 5 stock portfolios formed on *Index* using *FUN2012/FUN2022* functional. *Δ(FUN2012/FUN2022)* means the ratio of the return on the portfolio formed on *FUN2012* to the return on the portfolio formed on *FUN2022*. *Δ(FUN2012/Index)* means the ratio of the return on the portfolio formed on *FUN2012* to the return on the *Index*. *Δ(FUN2022/Index)* means the ratio of the return on the portfolio formed on *FUN2022* to the return on the *Index*.

Table A.2 SARIMA model parameters, base period, and prediction period for rolling differences between average returns and SR on 60 months, corresponding to the formed portfolios and the values of S&P 500 index

SARIMA parameters for season S= 12 months						*Base period*	*Prediction period*	*SARIMA coefficients*									
p	*d*	*q*	*P*	*D*	*Q*			*Const*	φ_1	φ_2	θ_1	θ_2	θ_3	Φ_1	Φ_2	Θ_1	Θ_2
Average returns differences																	
0	1	0				05.96-04.01	05.01-04.02										
0	1	0				05.96-04.02	05.02-04.03										
0	1	0				05.96-04.03	05.03-04.04										
0	1	0				05.96-04.04	05.04-04.05										
0	1	0				05.96-04.05	05.05-04.06										
2	2	1				05.96-04.06	05.06-04.07		-0.1127	0.1921	-0.9539						
0	2	1				05.96-04.07	05.07-04.08				-0.9638						
0	2	1				05.96-04.08	05.08-04.09				-0.9665						

(*Continued*)

Table A.2 (Continued)

SARIMA parameters for season S= 12 months						*Base period*	*Prediction period*	*SARIMA coefficients*									
p	d	q	P	D	Q			*Const*	φ_1	φ_2	θ_1	θ_2	θ_3	Φ_1	Φ_2	Θ_1	Θ_2
0	1	0	1	0	0	05.96-04.09	05.09-04.10							0.0412			
2	1	1	1	0	0	05.96-04.10	05.10-04.11		0.1936	0.2227	-0.2839			0.0312			
2	1	1	1	0	0	05.96-04.11	05.11-04.12		0.2112	0.2027	-0.2972			0.0292			
0	1	2	2	0	0	05.96-04.12	05.12-04.13				-0.0946	0.1439		0.0518	-0.0952		
0	1	2	2	0	0	05.96-04.13	05.13-04.14				-0.0813	0.1308		0.0534	-0.1145		
0	1	2	2	0	0	05.96-04.14	05.14-04.15				-0.0702	0.1392		0.0551	-0.0997		
0	1	2	2	0	0	05.96-04.15	05.15-04.16				-0.0665	0.1354		0.0566	-0.0850		
0	1	2	2	0	0	05.96-04.16	05.16-04.17				-0.0620	0.1342		0.0691	-0.0700		
0	1	2	2	0	0	05.96-04.17	05.17-04.18				-0.0675	0.1205		0.0634	-0.0907		

SR differences																
0	1	0				05.96-04.01	05.01-04.02	0.0039								
0	1	0				05.96-04.02	05.02-04.03	0.0031								
0	1	1				05.96-04.03	05.03-04.04	0.0028			0.2236					
0	1	1	0	0	1	05.96-04.04	05.04-04.05	0.0028			-0.2804					0.1711
0	2	2	0	0	1	05.96-04.05	05.05-04.06				-1.1442	0.1870				0.1613
2	2	1				05.96-04.06	05.06-04.07		-0.1901	-0.1408	-0.9273					
0	2	2				05.96-04.07	05.07-04.08							-1.1135	0.1588	
2	2	1				05.96-04.08	05.08-04.09		-0.1565	-0.1348	-0.9387					
0	2	2	0	0	1	05.96-04.09	05.09-04.10				-1.1737	0.2126				0.1422
0	2	2	0	0	1	05.96-04.10	05.10-04.11				-1.1642	0.2040				0.1245
2	2	1	0	0	1	05.96-04.11	05.11-04.12		-0.1803	-0.1259	-0.9436					0.1276
2	2	1	0	0	1	05.96-04.12	05.12-04.13		-0.1887	-0.1341	-0.9471					0.1379
0	2	3	0	0	1	05.96-04.13	05.13-04.14				-1.1240	0.0547	0.1120			0.1332

(*Continued*)

Table A.2 (Continued)

SARIMA parameters for season S= 12 months						*Base period*	*Prediction period*	*SARIMA coefficients*									
p	d	q	P	D	Q			*Const*	φ_1	φ_2	θ_1	θ_2	θ_3	Φ_1	Φ_2	Θ_1	Θ_2
0	2	2	0	0	1	05.96-04.14	05.14-04.15				-1.1025	0.1361				0.1323	
0	1	0	0	0	1	05.96-04.15	05.15-04.16									0.1452	
0	1	0	0	0	1	05.96-04.16	05.16-04.17									0.1411	
						05.96-04.17	05.17-04.18									0.1388	

Source: Own calculations using R-Studio ver. 4.2.3.

Notes: The parameters p,d,q correspond to ARIMA model while P,D,Q are related to its seasonal component. For more details see formula (37) and also formula (3.160) in Shumway and Stoffer (2011).

Table A.3 Holt–Winters method parameters, base period, and prediction period for rolling differences between average returns and SR on 60 months, corresponding to the formed portfolios and the values of S&P 500 index

Holt–Winters parameters		*Base period*	*Prediction period*
α	β		
Average returns differences			
0.96	0.07	05.96-04.01	05.01-04.02
0.95	0.08	05.96-04.02	05.02-04.03
0.96	0.06	05.96-04.03	05.03-04.04
0.93	0.06	05.96-04.04	05.04-04.05
0.93	0.08	05.96-04.05	05.05-04.06
0.88	0.1	05.96-04.06	05.06-04.07
0.9	0.09	05.96-04.07	05.07-04.08
0.92	0.08	05.96-04.08	05.08-04.09
0.9	0.08	05.96-04.09	05.09-04.10
0.9	0.08	05.96-04.10	05.10-04.11
0.9	0.08	05.96-04.11	05.11-04.12
0.9	0.07	05.96-04.12	05.12-04.13
0.91	0.07	05.96-04.13	05.13-04.14
0.93	0.06	05.96-04.14	05.14-04.15
0.93	0.06	05.96-04.15	05.15-04.16
0.93	0.06	05.96-04.16	05.16-04.17
0.93	0.06	05.96-04.17	05.17-04.18
SR differences			
0.86	0.07	05.96-04.01	05.01-04.02
0.83	0.07	05.96-04.02	05.02-04.03
0.79	0.05	05.96-04.03	05.03-04.04
0.75	0.05	05.96-04.04	05.04-04.05
0.82	0.06	05.96-04.05	05.05-04.06
0.8	0.07	05.96-04.06	05.06-04.07
0.84	0.06	05.96-04.07	05.07-04.08
0.84	0.06	05.96-04.08	05.08-04.09
0.79	0.06	05.96-04.09	05.09-04.10
0.8	0.06	05.96-04.10	05.10-04.11
0.82	0.06	05.96-04.11	05.11-04.12
0.81	0.06	05.96-04.12	05.12-04.13
0.82	0.06	05.96-04.13	05.13-04.14
0.88	0.05	05.96-04.14	05.14-04.15
0.89	0.05	05.96-04.15	05.15-04.16
0.89	0.05	05.96-04.16	05.16-04.17
0.89	0.05	05.96-04.17	05.17-04.18

Source: Own calculations using ITSM ver. 7.1.

Notes: α, β – for more details see formula (33 and 34) and Chatfield (1978).

Table A.4 SARIMA models parameters, base period, and prediction period for rolling differences between average returns and Sharpe ratios on 96 months, corresponding to the formed portfolios and the values of BE 500 index

SARIMA parameters for season S= 12 months						*Base period*	*Prediction period*	*SARIMA coefficients*								
P	*d*	*q*	*P*	*D*	*Q*			*Const*	φ_1	φ_2	θ_1	θ_2	Φ_1	Φ_2	Θ_1	Θ_2
Average returns differences																
1	1	1	0	0	1	05.01-04.09	05.09-04.10		0.7432 ***		-0.5266 ***				-0.5383 ***	
1	1	0	0	0	1	05.01-04.10	05.10-04.11		0.2658 ***						-0.5178 ***	
1	1	0	0	0	2	05.01-04.11	05.11-04.12		0.2253 **						-0.5277 ***	-0.1862
1	1	0	0	0	1	05.01-04.12	05.12-04.13		0.2975 ***						-0.5645 ***	
0	1	1	0	0	1	05.01-04.13	05.13-04.14				0.3054 ***				-0.5451 ***	
2	1	2	2	0	0	05.01-04.14	05.14-04.15		0.0203	0.3188 *	0.2663	-0.2838	-0.5005 ***	-0.2471 ***		

Average SR differences											
1	1	1	0	0	1	05.01-04.09	05.09-04.10	0.7499 ***	-0.5063 ***	-0.5453 ***	
1	1	1	0	0	1	05.01-04.10	05.10-04.11	0.7276 ***	-0.4793 ***	-0.546 ***	
1	1	0	0	0	2	05.01-04.11	05.11-04.12	0.2516 ***		-0.5411 ***	-0.2092 *
1	1	0	0	0	1	05.01-04.12	05.12-04.13	0.3967 ***		-0.5915 ***	
0	1	1	0	0	1	05.01-04.13	05.13-04.14		0.3594 ***	-0.5695 ***	
0	2	1	1	0	0	05.01-04.14	05.14-04.15	0.3100 ***	0.0911 ***	-0.6930 ***	

Notes: Significance of coefficients: ***p-value <0.01, **p-value<0.05, *p-value<0.1. The parameters p,d,q correspond to ARIMA model while P, D, Q are related to its seasonal component. For more details see formula (37) and also formula (3.160) in Shumway and Stoffer (2011).

Table A.5 Holt–Winters model parameters, base period, and prediction period for rolling differences between average returns and Sharpe ratios on 96 months, corresponding to the formed portfolios and the values of BE 500 index

Holt–Winters parameters		*Base period*	*Prediction period*
α	β		
Average returns difference			
1	0.15	05.2001-04.2009	05.2009-04.2010
1	0.23	05.2001-04.2010	05.2010-04.2011
1	0.19	05.2001-04.2011	05.2011-04.2012
1	0.27	05.2001-04.2012	05.2012-04.2013
1	0.13	05.2001-04.2013	05.2013-04.2014
1	0.1	05.2001-04.2014	05.2014-04.2015
Average Sharpe ratios difference			
1	0.17	05.2001-04.2009	05.2009-04.2010
1	0.28	05.2001-04.2010	05.2010-04.2011
1	0.22	05.2001-04.2011	05.2011-04.2012
1	0.43	05.2001-04.2012	05.2012-04.2013
1	0.24	05.2001-04.2013	05.2013-04.2014
1	0.02	05.2001-04.2014	05.2014-04.2015

Notes: α, β – for more details see formula (33 and 34) and Chatfield (1978).

Table A.6 SARIMA models parameters, base period, and prediction period for rolling differences between average returns and Sharpe ratios on 60 months, corresponding to the formed portfolios and the values of BE 500 index

SARIMA parameters for season S=12 months						*Base period*	*Prediction period*	*SARIMA coefficients*								
P	*d*	*q*	*P*	*D*	*Q*			*Const*	φ_1	φ_2	θ_1	θ_2	Φ_1	Φ_2	Θ_1	Θ_2
Average returns differences																
1	1	0	0	0	1	05.01-04.06	05.06-04.07	-0.0507	0.3249						-0.6504	
1	1	0	0	0	1	05.01-04.07	05.07-04.08	-0.0436	0.3251						-0.4314	
1	1	0	0	0	1	05.01-04.08	05.08-04.09		0.3764						-0.4032	
1	2	1	0	0	1	05.01-04.09	05.09-04.10		0.3216		-0.9208				-0.4634	
1	1	0	0	0	1	05.01-04.10	05.10-04.11		0.4053						-0.4848	
1	1	0	0	0	1	05.01-04.11	05.11-04.12		0.3690						-0.4590	
1	1	0	0	0	1	05.01-04.12	05.12-04.13		0.3489						-0.4467	
1	1	0	0	0	1	05.01-04.13	05.13-04.14		0.3447						-0.4503	
2	1	1	0	0	2	05.01-04.14	05.14-04.15		0.8689	-0.1067	-0.5870				-0.5951	-0.2135

(*Continued*)

Table A.6 (Continued)

SARIMA parameters for season S=12 months						*Base period*	*Prediction period*	*SARIMA coefficients*								
P	*d*	*q*	*P*	*D*	*Q*			*Const*	φ_1	φ_2	θ_1	θ_2	Φ_1	Φ_2	Θ_1	Θ_2
1	1	0	0	0	2	05.01-04.15	05.15-04.16		0.3252						-0.6064	-0.2337
1	0	1	2	0	0	05.01-04.16	05.16-04.17	1.4857	0.9800		0.3326				-0.4204	-0.1940
1	0	1	2	0	0	05.01-04.17	05.17-04.18	1.4990	0.9803		0.3186				-0.4364	-0.1979
Average SR differences																
1	1	0	0	0	1	05.01-04.06	05.06-04.07	-0.0088	0.3575						-0.7008	
1	1	0	0	0	1	05.01-04.07	05.07-04.08	0.3999							-0.4835	
1	1	1	0	0	1	05.01-04.08	05.08-04.09		0.7220		-0.4012				-0.4876	
1	1	0	0	0	1	05.01-04.09	05.09-04.10		0.4138						-0.4942	
1	1	1	0	0	1	05.01-04.10	05.10-04.11		0.7103		-0.3767				-0.5266	
1	1	0	0	0	1	05.01-04.11	05.11-04.12		0.3865						-0.5122	

1	1	0	0	0	1	05.01-04.12	05.12-04.13	0.3805	-0.5245
1	1	0	0	0	1	05.01-04.13	05.13-04.14	0.3664	-0.5167
1	1	0	0	0	1	05.01-04.14	05.14-04.15	0.3533	-0.5723
1	1	0	0	0	1	05.01-04.15	05.15-04.16	0.3574	-0.5941
1	1	0	0	0	1	05.01-04.16	05.16-04.17	0.3287	-0.5870
1	1	0	0	0	1	05.01-04.17	05.17-04.18	0.3171	-0.6079

Notes: The parameters p,d,q correspond to SARIMA model while P, D, Q are related to its seasonal component. For more details see formula (37) and also formula (3.160) in Shumway and Stoffer (2011).

Table A.7 Holt–Winters method parameters, base period, and prediction period for rolling differences between average returns and Sharpe ratios on 60 months, corresponding to the formed portfolios and the values of BE 500 index

Holt–Winters parameters		*Base period*	*Prediction period*
α	β		
Average returns difference			
1	0.4	05.01-04.06	05.06-04.07
1	0.38	05.01-04.07	05.07-04.08
1	0.35	05.01-04.08	05.08-04.09
1	0.29	05.01-04.09	05.09-04.10
1	0.31	05.01-04.10	05.10-04.11
1	0.31	05.01-04.11	05.11-04.12
1	0.3	05.01-04.12	05.12-04.13
1	0.27	05.01-04.13	05.13-04.14
1	0.26	05.01-04.14	05.14-04.15
1	0.27	05.01-04.15	05.15-04.16
1	0.22	05.01-04.16	05.16-04.17
1	0.2	05.01-04.17	05.17-04.18
Average Sharpe ratios difference			
1	0.43	05.01-04.06	05.06-04.07
1	0.42	05.01-04.07	05.07-04.08
1	0.41	05.01-04.08	05.08-04.09
1	0.38	05.01-04.09	05.09-04.10
1	0.39	05.01-04.10	05.10-04.11
1	0.38	05.01-04.11	05.11-04.12
1	0.37	05.01-04.12	05.12-04.13
1	0.33	05.01-04.13	05.13-04.14
1	0.31	05.01-04.14	05.14-04.15
1	0.34	05.01-04.15	05.15-04.16
1	0.29	05.01-04.16	05.16-04.17
1	0.27	05.01-04.17	05.17-04.18

Notes: α, β – for more details see formula (33 and 34) and Chatfield (1978).

Table A.8 SARIMA model parameters, base period, and prediction period for rolling differences between average returns and Sharpe ratios on 96 months, corresponding to the formed portfolios and the values of TOPIX 500 index

SARIMA parameters for season S= 12 months						*Base period*	*Prediction period*	*SARIMA coefficients*		
p	*d*	*q*	*P*	*D*	*Q*			*Const*	φ_2	θ_1
Average returns differences										
0	1	1	0	0	0	05.04-04.12	05.12-04.13			-0.2261 **
0	1	1	0	0	0	05.04-04.13	05.13-04.14			-0.2393 **
0	1	0	0	0	0	05.04-04.14	05.14-04.15			
Average SR differences										
1	1	0	0	0	0	05.04-04.12	05.12-04.13	-0.0013 *	-0.1573	
0	1	1	0	0	0	05.04-04.13	05.13-04.14	-0.0013 *		-0.1788 *
0	1	0	0	0	0	05.04-04.14	05.14-04.15			

Notes: Significance of coefficients: ***p-value <0.01, **p-value<0.05, *p-value<0.1. The parameters p,d,q correspond to ARIMA model while P, D, Q are related to its seasonal component. For more details see formula (37) and also formula (3.160) in Shumway and Stoffer (2011).

Table A.9 Holt–Winters model parameters, base period, and prediction period for rolling differences between average returns and Sharpe ratios on 96 months, corresponding to the formed portfolios and the values of TOPIX 500 index

Holt–Winters parameters		*Base period*	*Prediction period*
α	β		
Average returns difference			
0.79	0.03	05.2004-04.2012	05.2012-04.2013
0.78	0.03	05.2004-04.2013	05.2013-04.2014
0.85	0.02	05.2004-04.2014	05.2014-04.2015
Average Sharpe ratios difference			
0.87	0.03	05.2004-04.2012	05.2012-04.2013
0.85	0.03	05.2004-04.2013	05.2013-04.2014
0.87	0.03	05.2004-04.2014	05.2014-04.2015

Notes: α, β – for more details see formula (33 and 34) and Chatfield (1978).

Table A.10 SARIMA model parameters, base period, and prediction period for rolling differences between average returns and Sharpe ratios on 60 months, corresponding to the formed portfolios and the values of TOPIX 500 index

SARIMA parameters for season S=12 months						*Base period*	*Prediction period*	*SARIMA coefficients*		
p	*d*	*q*	*P*	*D*	*Q*			*Const*	φ_2	θ_1
Average returns differences										
0	1	0				05.04-04.09	05.09-04.10			
0	1	0				05.04-04.10	05.10-04.11			
0	1	0				05.04-04.11	05.11-04.12			
0	1	0				05.04-04.12	05.12-04.13			
0	1	0				05.04-04.13	05.13-04.14			
0	1	0				05.04-04.14	05.14-04.15			
0	1	0				05.04-04.15	05.15-04.16			
0	1	0				05.04-04.16	05.16-04.17			
0	1	0				05.04-04.17	05.17-04.18			
Average SR differences										
0	1	0				05.04-04.09	05.09-04.10			
0	1	0				05.04-04.10	05.10-04.11			
0	1	0				05.04-04.11	05.11-04.12			
0	1	0			0	05.04-04.12	05.12-04.13			
0	1	0			0	05.04-04.13	05.13-04.14			
0	1	0			0	05.04-04.14	05.14-04.15			
0	1	0				05.04-04.15	05.15-04.16			
0	1	0				05.04-04.16	05.16-04.17			
0	1	0				05.04-04.17	05.17-04.18			

Notes: The parameters *p,d,q* correspond to ARIMA model while.

Table A.11 Holt–Winters model parameters, base period, and prediction period for rolling differences between average returns and Sharpe ratios on 60 months, corresponding to the formed portfolios and the values of TOPIX 500 index

Holt–Winters parameters		*Base period*	*Prediction period*
α	β		
Average returns difference			
0.96	0.12	05.04-04.09	05.09-04.10
0.99	0.1	05.04-04.10	05.10-04.11
0.92	0.1	05.04-04.11	05.11-04.12
0.92	0.1	05.04-04.12	05.12-04.13
1	0.08	05.04-04.13	05.13-04.14
1	0.07	05.04-04.14	05.14-04.15
0.97	0.07	05.04-04.15	05.15-04.16
0.97	0.07	05.04-04.16	05.16-04.17
1	0.07	05.04-04.17	05.17-04.18
Average Sharpe ratios difference			
0.89	0.09	05.04-04.09	05.09-04.10
0.92	0.06	05.04-04.10	05.10-04.11
0.86	0.05	05.04-04.11	05.11-04.12
0.88	0.04	05.04-04.12	05.12-04.13
0.96	0.03	05.04-04.13	05.13-04.14
0.98	0.03	05.04-04.14	05.14-04.15
1	0.03	05.04-04.15	05.15-04.16
0.98	0.02	05.04-04.16	05.16-04.17
1	0.02	05.04-04.17	05.17-04.18

Notes: α, β – for more details see formula (33 and 34) and Chatfield (1978).

Table A.12 SARIMA model parameters, base period, and prediction period for rolling differences between average returns and Sharpe ratios on 96 months, corresponding to the formed portfolios and the values of SSE 380 index

SARIMA parameters for season S=12 months						*Base period*	*Prediction period*	*SARIMA coefficients*		
p	*d*	*q*	*P*	*D*	*Q*			*Const*	φ_2	θ_1
Average returns differences										
0	1	1	0	0	0	05.03-04.11	05.11-04.12	0.0154**		-0.6445***
0	1	1	0	0	0	05.03-04.12	05.12-04.13	0.0117**		-0.6282***
0	1	1	0	0	0	05.03-04.13	05.13-04.14			-0.5500***
1	1	1	0	0	0	05.03-04.14	05.14-04.15	0.0102*	0.3426*	-0.7660***
Average SR differences										
0	1	1	0	0	0	05.03-04.11	05.11-04.12	0,0023***		-0.6278***
0	1	1	0	0	0	05.03-04.12	05.12-04.13	0.0015**		-0.6132***
0	1	1	0	0	0	05.03-04.13	05.13-04.14	0.0011		-0.5604***
0	1	1	0	0	0	05.03-04.14	05.14-04.15			-0.5064***

Notes: Significance of coefficients: ***p-value <0.01, **p-value<0.05, *p-value<0.1. The parameters p,d,q correspond to ARIMA model while P, D, Q are related to its seasonal component. For more details see formula (37) and also formula (3.160) in Shumway and Stoffer (2011).

Table A.13 Holt–Winters method parameters, base period, and prediction period for rolling differences between average returns and Sharpe ratios on 96 months, corresponding to the formed portfolios and the values of SSE 380 index

Holt–Winters parameters		*Base period*	*Prediction period*
α	β		
Average returns difference			
0.5	0.08	05.2003-04.2011	05.2011-04.2012
0.5	0.08	05.2003-04.2012	05.2012-04.2013
0.49	0.08	05.2003-04.2013	05.2013-04.2014
0.61	0.05	05.2003-04.2014	05.2014-04.2015
Average Sharpe ratios difference			
0.45	0.08	05.2003-04.2011	05.2011-04.2012
0.47	0.08	05.2003-04.2012	05.2012-04.2013
0.44	0.1	05.2003-04.2013	05.2013-04.2014
0.52	0.06	05.2003-04.2014	05.2014-04.2015

Notes: α, β – for more details see formula (33 and 34) and Chatfield (1978).

Table A.14 SARIMA model parameters, base period, and prediction period for rolling differences between average returns and Sharpe ratios on 60 months, corresponding to the formed portfolios and the values of SSE 380 index

SARIMA parameters for season S= 12 months						*Base period*	*Prediction period*	*SARIMA coefficients*									
p	*d*	*q*	*P*	*D*	*Q*			*Const.*	φ_1	φ_2	θ_1	θ_2	θ_3	θ_4	Φ_1	Φ_2	Θ_1
Average returns differences																	
0	1	1				05.03-04.08	05.08-04.09				-0.5726						
0	1	1				05.03-04.09	05.09-04.10				-0.5453						
0	1	1				05.03-04.10	05.10-04.11				-0.5198						
0	1	1				05.03-04.11	05.11-04.12				-0.4783						
0	1	1				05.03-04.12	05.12-04.13				-0.4867						
0	1	1				05.03-04.13	05.13-04.14				-0.4829						
0	1	1				05.03-04.14	05.14-04.15	0.0181			-0.5143						
0	1	1				05.03-04.15	05.15-04.16				-0.4755						

(*Continued*)

Table A.14 (Continued)

SARIMA parameters for season S= 12 months						*Base period*	*Prediction period*	*SARIMA coefficients*									
p	*d*	*q*	*P*	*D*	*Q*			*Const.*	φ_1	φ_2	θ_1	θ_2	θ_3	θ_4	Φ_1	Φ_2	Θ_1
2	1	3	1	0	0	05.03-04.16	05.16-04.17		-1.0779	-0.6268	0.7388	0.2228	-0.4833		0.0732		
0	1	3	1	0	0	05.03-04.17	05.17-04.18				-0.3280	-0.0496	-0.1606		0.1422		
Average SR differences																	
0	1	1				05.03-04.08	05.08-04.09				-0.5895						
1	1	0				05.03-04.09	05.09-04.10		-0.5551								
0	1	1				05.03-04.10	05.10-04.11				-0.5645						
0	1	1				05.03-04.11	05.11-04.12				-0.5251						
0	1	1				05.03-04.12	05.12-04.13				-0.5286						

0	1	1				05.03-04.13	05.13-04.14	0.0016			-0.5708				
0	1	1				05.03-04.14	05.14-04.15	0.0019			-0.5721				
0	1	1				05.03-04.15	05.15-04.16	0.0014			-0.5538				
0	1	4	1	0	0	05.03-04.16	05.16-04.17				-0.3712	-0.1317	-0.2645	0.2856	0.1569
0	1	3	1	0	0	05.03-04.17	05.17-04.18				-0.3741	-0.0696	-0.1423		0.1635

Notes: The parameters *p,d,q* correspond to ARIMA model while *P, D, Q* are related to its seasonal component. For more details see formula (37) and also formula (3.160) in Shumway and Stoffer (2011).

Table A.15 Holt–Winters method parameters, base period, and prediction period for rolling differences between average returns and Sharpe ratios on 60 months, corresponding to the formed portfolios and the values of SSE 380 index

Holt–Winters parameters		*Base period*	*Prediction period*
α	β		
Average returns difference			
0.49	0.24	05.03-04.08	05.08-04.09
0.49	0.24	05.03-04.09	05.09-04.10
0.52	0.22	05.03-04.10	05.10-04.11
0.62	0.09	05.03-04.11	05.11-04.12
0.61	0.09	05.03-04.12	05.12-04.13
0.62	0.08	05.03-04.13	05.13-04.14
0.61	0.08	05.03-04.14	05.14-04.15
0.61	0.08	05.03-04.15	05.15-04.16
0.62	0.08	05.03-04.16	05.16-04.17
0.68	0.06	05.03-04.17	05.17-04.18
Average Sharpe ratios difference			
0.46	0.32	05.03-04.08	05.08-04.09
0.46	0.28	05.03-04.09	05.09-04.10
0.49	0.24	05.03-04.10	05.10-04.11
0.59	0.1	05.03-04.11	05.11-04.12
0.58	0.1	05.03-04.12	05.12-04.13
0.58	0.09	05.03-04.13	05.13-04.14
0.57	0.09	05.03-04.14	05.14-04.15
0.58	0.09	05.03-04.15	05.15-04.16
0.58	0.09	05.03-04.16	05.16-04.17
0.61	0.07	05.03-04.17	05.17-04.18

Notes: α, β – for more details see formula (33 and 34) and Chatfield (1978).

Table A.16 SARIMA model parameters, base period, and prediction period for rolling differences between average returns and Sharpe ratios on 96 months, corresponding to the formed portfolios and the values of WIG index

SARIMA parameters for season S= 12 months	*Base period*	*Prediction period*	*SARIMA coefficients*								
			Const	φ_1	φ_2	θ_1	θ_2	θ_3	Θ_1	Φ_1	Φ_2
Average returns differences											
0 2 2 1 0 0	05.96-04.04	05.04-04.05				-0.6634 ***	-0.2811 ***			0.1922 *	
0 2 2 1 0 0	05.96-04.05	05.05-04.06				-0.6622 ***	-0.2977 ***			0.2010 **	
0 2 2 1 0 0	05.96-04.06	05.06-04.07				-0.6690 ***	-0.2899 ***			0.1843 **	
2 2 1 0 0 1	05.96-04.07	05.07-04.08		0.2174 **	-0.1515	-0.9317 ***					0.1504
0 2 2	05.96-04.08	05.08-04.09				-0.6691 ***	-0.2825 ***				
0 1 1	05.96-04.09	05.09-04.10				0.3637 ***					
0 1 1	05.96-04.10	05.10-04.11				0.3599 ***					
0 1 1	05.96-04.11	05.11-04.12				0.3496 ***					
0 1 1	05.96-04.12	05.12-04.13				0.3625 ***					

(*Continued*)

Table A.16 (Continued)

SARIMA parameters for season S= 12 months	*Base period*	*Prediction period*	*SARIMA coefficients*								
			Const	φ_1	φ_2	θ_1	$\Theta_2 \theta_2$	θ_3	Θ_1	Φ_1	Φ_2
0 1 1	05.96-04.13	05.13-04.14				0.3842 ***					
0 1 1	05.96-04.14	05.14-04.15				0.3847 ***					
Average SR differences											
2 2 1 1 0 0	05.96-04.04	05.04-04.05		-0.2250 **	-0.2851 ***	-0.9274 ***				0.2225 **	
2 2 1 1 0 0	05.96-04.05	05.05-04.06		-0.2174 **	-0.2814 ***	-0.9307 ***				0.2385 **	
2 1 2 1 0 0	05.96-04.06	05.06-04.07		-0.2195	-0.6880	0.0566	0.4899 *			0.2624 **	
2 2 1 0 0 1	05.96-04.07	05.07-04.08		-0.2166 **	-0.2671 ***	-0.9302 ***					0.2082 **
0 1 1 1 0 0	05.96-04.08	05.08-04.09				-0.1847 **				0.2270 ***	
2 1 2 1 0 0	05.96-04.09	05.09-04.10		-0.3319 **	-0.8046 ***	0.1801	0.5331 ***			0.2658 ***	
2 1 2 1 0 0	05.96-04.10	05.10-04.11		-0.2895 **	-0.7683 ***	0.1624	0.5025 **			0.2240 ***	

2	1	3	1	0	0	05.96-04.11	05.11-04.12	-0.3679 ***	-0.8160 ***	0.1997	0.5454 **	-0.1086	0.2441 ***		
2	1	0	0	0	2	05.96-04.12	05.12-04.13	-0.1446 **	-0.3795 ***					0.1735 **	0.1787 **
2	1	2	1	0	0	05.96-04.13	05.13-04.14	-0.3310 ***	-0.8217 ***	0.2830 **	0.5725 ***		0.2259 ***		
2	1	2	0	0	2	05.96-04.14	05.14-04.15	-0.2791 **	-0.7469 ***	0.1962	0.4926 ***			0.1654 **	0.1815 **

Notes: Significance of coefficients: ***p-value <0.01, **p-value<0.05, *p-value<0.1. The parameters p,d,q correspond to ARIMA model while P, D, Q are related to its seasonal component. For more details see formula (37) and also formula (3.160) in Shumway and Stoffer (2011).

Table A.17 Holt–Winters method parameters, base period, and prediction period for rolling differences between average returns and Sharpe ratios on 96 months, corresponding to the formed portfolios and the values of WIG index

Holt–Winters parameters		*Base period*	*Prediction period*
α	β		
Average returns difference			
1	0.08	05.1996-04.2004	05.2004-04.2005
1	0.08	05.1996-04.2005	05.2005-04.2006
1	0.07	05.1996-04.2006	05.2006-04.2007
1	0.09	05.1996-04.2007	05.2007-04.2008
1	0.08	05.1996-04.2008	05.2008-04.2009
1	0.13	05.1996-04.2009	05.2009-04.2010
1	0.14	05.1996-04.2010	05.2010-04.2011
1	0.14	05.1996-04.2011	05.2011-04.2012
1	0.12	05.1996-04.2012	05.2012-04.2013
1	0.1	05.1996-04.2013	05.2013-04.2014
1	0.09	05.1996-04.2014	05.2014-04.2015
Average Sharpe ratios difference			
0.72	0.08	05.1996-04.2004	05.2004-04.2005
0.75	0.07	05.1996-04.2005	05.2005-04.2006
0.74	0.07	05.1996-04.2006	05.2006-04.2007
0.74	0.07	05.1996-04.2007	05.2007-04.2008
0.75	0.07	05.1996-04.2008	05.2008-04.2009
0.71	0.06	05.1996-04.2009	05.2009-04.2010
0.68	0.06	05.1996-04.2010	05.2010-04.2011
0.69	0.06	05.1996-04.2011	05.2011-04.2012
0.71	0.05	05.1996-04.2012	05.2012-04.2013
0.76	0.05	05.1996-04.2013	05.2013-04.2014
0.8	0.04	05.1996-04.2014	05.2014-04.2015

Notes: α, β – for more details see formula (33 and 34) and Chatfield (1978).

Table A.18 SARIMA model parameters, base period, and prediction period for rolling differences between average returns and Sharpe ratios on 60 months, corresponding to the formed portfolios and the values of WIG index

SARIMA parameters for season S= 12 months						*Base period*	*Prediction period*	*SARIMA coefficients*									
p	*d*	*Q*	*P*	*D*	*Q*			*Const*	φ_1	φ_2	φ_3	θ_1	θ_2	θ_3	θ_4	Φ_1	Θ_1
Average returns differences																	
0	1	1				05.96-04.01	05.01-04.02	0.0535				-0.3363					
0	1	1	1	0	0	05.96-04.02	05.02-04.03	0.0646				-0.2110				-0.2167	
0	1	1				05.96-04.03	05.03-04.04	0.0471				-0.1946					
0	1	0				05.96-04.04	05.04-04.05										
0	2	1				05.96-04.05	05.05-04.06					-0.9657					
0	2	1				05.96-04.06	05.06-04.07					-0.9650					
0	2	1				05.96-04.07	05.07-04.08					-0.9589					
0	2	1				05.96-04.08	05.08-04.09					-0.9669					

(*Continued*)

Table A.18 (Continued)

SARIMA parameters for season S= 12 months						Base period	Prediction period	SARIMA coefficients									
p	*d*	*Q*	*P*	*D*	*Q*			*Const*	φ_1	φ_2	φ_3	θ_1	θ_2	θ_3	θ_4	Φ_1	Θ_1
0	2	1				05.96-04.09	05.09-04.10					-0.9709					
0	2	1				05.96-04.10	05.10-04.11					-0.9728					
0	2	1				05.96-04.11	05.11-04.12					-0.9739					
0	1	0				05.96-04.12	05.12-04.13										
0	1	0				05.96-04.13	05.13-04.14										
0	1	0				05.96-04.14	05.14-04.15										
0	1	0				05.96-04.15	05.15-04.16										
0	1	0				05.96-04.16	05.16-04.17										
0	1	0				05.96-04.17	05.17-04.18										

SR differences

0	1	1	1	0	0	05.96-04.01	05.01-04.02	0.0069				-0.5205				-0.2358
0	1	1	1	0	0	05.96-04.02	05.02-04.03	0.0043				-0.2148				-0.2632
0	2	2				05.96-04.03	05.03-04.04					-1.2908	0.3484			
0	2	2				05.96-04.04	05.04-04.05					-1.3504	0.4052			
0	2	3				05.96-04.05	05.05-04.06					-1.2793	0.1795	0.1527		
3	2	1				05.96-04.06	05.06-04.07		-0.3516	-0.2942	-0.1525	-0.9135				
3	2	1				05.96-04.07	05.07-04.08		-0.3611	-0.3242	-0.1680	-0.9150				
3	2	1				05.96-04.08	05.08-04.09		-0.3488	-0.2875	-0.1552	-0.9242				
2	2	1				05.96-04.09	05.09-04.10		-0.2782	-0.2906		-0.9452				
3	2	1				05.96-04.10	05.10-04.11		-0.3315	-0.3555	-0.1643	-0.9281				
0	1	4				05.96-04.11	05.11-04.12					-0.243	-0.1970	0.0272	0.1736	

(*Continued*)

Table A.18 (Continued)

SARIMA parameters for season S= 12 months						*Base period*	*Prediction period*	*SARIMA coefficients*									
p	*d*	*Q*	*P*	*D*	*Q*			*Const*	φ_1	φ_2	φ_3	θ_1	θ_2	θ_3	θ_4	Φ_1	Θ_1
0	1	4				05.96-04.12	05.12-04.13					-0.2261	-0.1931	0.0208	0.1552		
1	1	3				05.96-04.13	05.13-04.14		0.9394			-1.1994	0.0467	0.2323			
1	1	3				05.96-04.14	05.14-04.15		0.9348			-1.2060	0.0442	0.2459			
2	1	0				05.96-04.15	05.15-04.16		-0.1944	-0.2623							
2	1	0				05.96-04.16	05.16-04.17		-0.1783	-0.2329							
2	1	0				05.96-04.17	05.17-04.18		-0.1716	-0.2341							

Notes: The parameters *p,d,q* correspond to ARIMA model while *P, D, Q* are related to its seasonal component. For more details see formula (37) and also formula (3.160) in Shumway and Stoffer (2011).

Table A.19 Holt–Winters method parameters, base period, and prediction period for rolling differences between average returns and Sharpe ratios on 60 months, corresponding to the formed portfolios and the values of WIG index

Holt–Winters parameters		*Base period*	*Prediction period*
α	β		
Average returns differences			
0.66	0.12	05.96-04.01	05.01-04.02
0.73	0.14	05.96-04.02	05.02-04.03
0.83	0.06	05.96-04.03	05.03-04.04
0.87	0.06	05.96-04.04	05.04-04.05
0.87	0.06	05.96-04.05	05.05-04.06
0.88	0.05	05.96-04.06	05.06-04.07
0.86	0.06	05.96-04.07	05.07-04.08
0.9	0.04	05.96-04.08	05.08-04.09
0.96	0.03	05.96-04.09	05.09-04.10
0.96	0.03	05.96-04.10	05.10-04.11
0.95	0.03	05.96-04.11	05.11-04.12
0.95	0.03	05.96-04.12	05.12-04.13
0.99	0.01	05.96-04.13	05.13-04.14
0.98	0.01	05.96-04.14	05.14-04.15
0.99	0.01	05.96-04.15	05.15-04.16
0.99	0.02	05.96-04.16	05.16-04.17
1	0.01	05.96-04.17	05.17-04.18
SR differences			
0.51	0.16	05.96-04.01	05.01-04.02
0.67	0.12	05.96-04.02	05.02-04.03
0.66	0.11	05.96-04.03	05.03-04.04
0.59	0.12	05.96-04.04	05.04-04.05
0.62	0.1	05.96-04.05	05.05-04.06
0.62	0.1	05.96-04.06	05.06-04.07
0.6	0.1	05.96-04.07	05.07-04.08
0.63	0.08	05.96-04.08	05.08-04.09
0.62	0.08	05.96-04.09	05.09-04.10
0.6	0.08	05.96-04.10	05.10-04.11
0.6	0.08	05.96-04.11	05.11-04.12
0.64	0.07	05.96-04.12	05.12-04.13
0.67	0.06	05.96-04.13	05.13-04.14
0.66	0.06	05.96-04.14	05.14-04.15
0.66	0.06	05.96-04.15	05.15-04.16
0.7	0.05	05.96-04.16	05.16-04.17
0.76	0.03	05.96-04.17	05.17-04.18

Notes: α, β – for more details see formula (33 and 34) and Chatfield (1978)

References

Chatfield, C. (1978). The Holt-Winters Forecasting Procedure. Applied Statistics 27 (3), 264–279.

Shumway, R.H., & Stoffer, D.S. (2011). *Time Series Analysis and Its Applications. With R Examples*. 3rd ed. New York: Springer.

References

Abbott, W.F., & Monsen, R.J. (1979). On the Measurement of Corporate Social Responsibility: Self-Reported Disclosures as a Method of Measuring Corporate Social Involvement. *Academy of Management Journal* 22 (3), 501–515.

Agrawal, G. (2007). Monetary Policy Announcements and Stock Price Behavior: Empirical Evidence from CNX Nifty. *Decision* 34 (2), 133–153.

Alexander, G.J., & Buchholz, R.A. (1978). Corporate Social Responsibility and Stock Market Performance. *Academy of Management Journal* 21 (3), 479–486.

Ali, S.B., Farooq, K., Shah, Z.A., & Burney, S. (2021). Testing the Evidence on Weak Form EMH at Pakistan Stock Market. *Turkish Online Journal of Qualitative Inquiry (TOJQI)* 12 (8), 5147–5153.

Ameer, S., Nor, S.M., Ali, S., Zawawi, & N.H.M. (2023). The Impact of COVID-19 on BRICS and MSCI Emerging Markets Efficiency: Evidence from MF-DFA. *Fractal and Fractional* 7, 519.

Anderson, J.C., & Frankle, A.W. (1980). Voluntary Social Reporting: As Iso-Beta Portfolio Analysis. *The Accounting Review* LV (3), 468–479.

Aupperle, K.E., Carroll, A.B., & Hatfield, J.D. (1985). An Empirical Examination of the Relationship Between Corporate Social Responsibility and Profitability. *Academy of Management Journal* 28 (2), 446–463.

Basu, S. (1977). Investment Performance of Common Stocks in Relation to Their Price-Earnings Ratios: A Test of the Efficient Market Hypothesis. *Journal of Finance* 32 (3), 663–682.

Belkaoui, A. (1976). The Impact of the Disclosure of the Environmental Effects of Organizational Behavior on the Market. *Financial Management* 5 (4), 26–31.

Belkaoui, A., & Karpik, P. (1989). Determinants of the Corporate Decision to Disclose Social Information. *Accounting, Auditing and Accountability Journal* 2 (1), 36–51.

Blackburn, V., Doran, M., & Shrader, C.B. (1994). Investigating the Dimensions of Social Responsibility and the Consequences for Corporate Financial Performance. *Journal of Managerial Issues* 6 (2, Summer), 195–212.

Boldt, B.L., & Arbit, H.L. (1984). Efficient Markets and Professional Investor. *Financial Analysts Journal* 40 (4), 22–34.

Bowman, E., & Haire, M. (1975). A Strategic Posture Toward Corporate Social Responsibility. *California Management Review* XVIII (2), 49–58.

Bragdon, J.H., & Marlin, J.A. (1972). Is Pollution Profitable? *Risk Management* 19 (4), 9–18.

Brine, M., Brown, R., & Hackett, G. (2006). Corporate Social Responsibility and Financial Performance in the Australian Context. *Economic Round-up, Autumn* 2007, 47–58.

Buehler, V.M., & Shetty, Y.K. (1976). Managerial Response to Social Responsibility Challenge. *Academy of Management Journal* 19 (1), 66–78.

Bulski, D., & Górski, M. (2012). Wyniki testów hipotezy półsilnej efektywności informacyjnej Giełdy Papierów Wartościowych w Warszawie w latach 2005–2011. *Problemy Zarządzania* 10/4 (1), 141–168.

Carhart, M.M. (1997). On Persistence in Mutual Fund Performance. *Journal of Finance* 52 (1), 57–82.

Cellier, A., & Chollet, P. (2011). *The Impact of Corporate Social Responsibility Rating Announcements on European Stock Prices. International Conference of the French Finance Association (AFFI), May 11–13, 2011.*

Chaboud, A., Chiquoine, B., Hjalmarsson, E., & Vega, C. (2009). Rise of the Machines: Algorithmic Trading in the Foreign Exchange Market. Board of Governors of the Federal Reserve System. *International Finance Discussion Papers* 980, 1–44.

Chatfield, C. (1978). The Holt-Winters Forecasting Procedure. *Applied Statistics* 27 (3), 264–279.

Cheng, B., Ioannou, I., & Serafeim, G. (2014). Corporate Social Responsibility and Access to Finance. *Strategic Management Journal* 35, 1–23.

Chou, P.-H., & Zhou, G. (2006). Using Bootstrap to Test Portfolio Efficiency. *Annals of Economics and Finance* 7 (2), 217–249.

Chu, S.F., & Lim, G.H. (1998). Share Performance and Profit Efficiency of Banks in an Oligopolistic Market: Evidence from Singapore. *Journal of Multinational Financial Management* 8, 155–168.

Cochrane, J. (2001). *Asset Pricing*. Princeton, NJ: Princeton University Press.

Converse, N., Levy-Yeyati, E., & Williams, T. (2023). How ETFs Amplify the Global Financial Cycle in Emerging Markets. *Review of Financial Studies* 36 (9), 3423–3462.

Di Donato, F., & Izzo, M.F. (2012). The Relation between Corporate Social Responsibility and Stock Prices: An Analysis of the Italian Listed Companies, https://papers.ssrn.com/sol3/Delivery.cfm/SSRN_ID1986324_code907333.pdf?abstractid=1986324&mirid=1 (Accessed October 30, 2017).

Dobrescu, D. (2013). The Impact of Corporate Social Responsibility on Corporate Value. *USV Annals of Economics and Public Administration* 13 (2), 91–101.

Duhigg, C. (2009). Stock Traders Find Speed Pays, in Milliseconds. *New York Times*, July 23.

Endrikat, J., Guenther, E., & Hoppe, H. (2014). Making Sense of Conflicting Empirical Findings: A Meta-Analytic Review of the Relationship Between Corporate Environmental and Financial Performance. *European Management Journal* 32, 735–751.

European Commission (2019). *Communication from the Commission to the European Parliament, the Council, the European Economic and Social Committee and the Committee of the Regions*. COM(2019) 640 final. Brussels: The European Green Deal.

Fama, E.F. (1965a). The Behavior of Stock-Market Prices. *Journal of Business* 38 (1), 34–105.

Fama, E.F. (1965b). Random Walks in Stock-Market Prices. *Financial Analysts Journal* 21 (5), 55–59.

Fama, E.F. (1970). Efficient Capital Markets: A Review of Theory and Empirical Work. *Journal of Finance* 25 (2), 383–417.

Fama, E.F. (1991). Efficient Capital Market: II. *Journal of Finance* 46 (5), 1575–1617.

Fama, E.F., Fisher, L., Jensen, M.C., & Roll, R. (1969). The Adjustment of Stock Prices to New Information. *International Economic Review* 10 (1), 1–21.

Fama, E.F., & French, K.R. (1993). Common Risk Factors in the Returns on Stocks and Bonds. *Journal of Financial Economics* 33, 3–56.

Fama, E.F., & French, K.R. (1995). Size and Book-to-Market Factors in Earnings and Returns. *The Journal of Finance* 50 (1), 131–155.

Fiori, G., di Donato, F., & Izzo, M.F. (2007). *Corporate Social Responsibility and Firms Performance – An Analysis on Italian Listed Companies.* https://papers.ssrn.com/sol3/papers.cfm?abstract_id=1032851 (Accessed November 2, 2017).

Fogler, H.R., & Nutt, F. (1975). A Note on Social Responsibility and Stock Valuation. *Academy of Management Journal* 18 (1), 155–160.

Fry, F., & Hock, R. (1976). Who Claims Corporate Responsibility? The Biggest and the Worst. *Business and Society Review* 18 (18), 62–65.

Fuller, R.J., & Farrell, J.L. (1987). *Modern Investments and Security Analysis*. New York: McGraw-Hill.

Galbreath, J. (2006). Does Primary Stakeholder Management Positively Affect the Bottom Line?: Some Evidence from Australia. *Management Decision* 44 (8), 1106–1121.

Gibbons, M.R., Ross, S.A., & Shanken, J. (1989). A Test of the Efficiency of a Given Portfolio. *Econometrica* 57 (5), 1121–1152.

Godfrey, P.C., Merrill, C.B., & Hansen, J.M. (2009). The Relationship Between Corporate Social Responsibility and Shareholder Value: An Empirical Test of the Risk Management Hypothesis. *Strategic Management Journal* 30 (4), 425–445.

Goel, A., & Sahay, N. (2023). Investigating the Market Efficiency of Socially Responsible Indices: Evidence from India. *International Journal of Finance, Economics and Business* 2 (4), 301–312.

Goss, B.A., Avsar, S.G., & Chan, S.-C. (1992). Rational Expectations and Price Determination in the US Oats Market. *Economic Record* 68, 16–26.

Greene, W.H. (2003). *Econometric Analysis*. Upper Saddle River, NJ: Prentice Hall.

Gregory, A., Tharyan, R., & Whittaker, J. (2014). Corporate Social Responsibility and Firm Value: Disaggregating the Effects on Cash Flow, Risk and Growth. *Journal of Business Ethics* 124 (4), 633–657.

Groenewold, N. (1997). Share Market Efficiency: Tests Using Daily Data for Australia and New Zealand. *Applied Financial Economics* 7 (6), 645–657.

Grossman, S.J., & Stiglitz, J.E. (1980). On the Impossibility of Informationally Efficient Markets. *American Economic Review* 70 (3), 393–408.

Gupta, D., Anand, A., & Singh, R. (2008). Empirical Testing of Strong Form of Market Efficiency. *Asia-Pacific Business Review* 4 (3), 53–59.

Gurgul, H., Mittere, C., & Wójtowicz, T. (2021). The Impact of US Macroeconomic News on the Prices of Single Stocks on the Vienna Stock Exchange. *Central European Journal of Economic Modelling and Econometrics* 13, 287–329.

Gurung, P., & Sarkar, S. (2023). Testing of Market Efficiency of BSE GREENEX: An Empirical Analysis. *SDMIMD Journal of Management* 14 (1), 91–106.

Hart, S.L., & Ahuja, G. (1996). Does it Pat to be Green? An Empirical Examination of the Relationship Between Emission Reduction and Firm Performance. *Business Strategy and the Environment* 5, 30–37.

Hendershott, T., & Riordan, R. (2009). *Algorithmic Trading and Information*. Working Papers 09-08, NET Institute.

Hotelling, H. (1933). Analysis of a Complex of Statistical Variables into Principal Components. *Journal of Educational Psychology* 24, 417–441.

Hung, J.-C., Lee, Y.-H., & Pai, T.-Y. (2009). Examining Market Efficiency for Large- and Small-Capitalization of TOPIX and FTSE Stock Indices. *Applied Financial Economics* 19, 735–744.

Ingram, R. (1978). An Investigation of the Information Content of (Certain) Social Responsibility Disclosures. *Journal of Accounting Research* 16 (2), 270–285.

Inoue, Y., & Lee, S. (2011). Effects of Different Dimensions of Corporate Social Responsibility on Corporate Financial Performance in Tourism-Related Industries. *Tourism Management* 32, 790–804.

Investment Company Institute (2023). *Investment Company Fact Book. A Review of Trends and Activities in the Investment Company Industry.* www.ici.org/system/files/2023-05/2023-factbook.pdf (Accessed March 25, 2025)

Jaffe, J.F. (1974). Special Information and Insider Trading. *Journal of Business* 47 (3), 410–428.

Jensen, M.C. (1978). Some Anomalous Evidence Regarding Market Efficiency. *Journal of Financial Economics 6* (2/3), 95–101.

Johnson, R.A., & Greening, D.W. (1999). The Effects of Corporate Governance and Institutional Ownership Types on Corporate Social Performance. *Academy of Management Journal* 42 (5), 564–576.

Khan, A.Q., & Ikram, S. (2010). Testing Semi-Strong Form of Efficient Market Hypothesis in Relation to the Impact of Foreign Institutional Investors' (FII's) Investments on Indian Capital Market. *International Journal of Trade, Economics and Finance* 1 (4), 373–379.

Kubacki, D. (2017). Porównanie efektywności informacyjnej rynku finansowego w wybranych krajach Unii Europejskiej. *Finanse, Rynki Finansowe, Ubezpieczenia* 2/2017 (86), 123–133.

Lener, L.D., & Fryxell, G.E. (1988). An Empirical Study of the Predictors of Corporate Social Performance: A Multi-Dimensional Analysis. *Journal of Business Ethics* 7 (12), 951–959.

Leuthold, R.M., & Hartmann, P.A. (1979). A Semi-Strong Form Evaluation of the Efficiency of the Hog Futures Market. *American Journal of Agricultural Economics* 61 (3), 482–489.

Leuthold, R.M., & Hartmann, P.A. (1980). A Semi-Strong Form Evaluation of the Efficiency of the Hog Futures Market: Reply. *American Journal of Agricultural Economics* 62 (3), 585–587.

Lintner, J. (1965). The Valuation of Risk Assets and the Selection of Risky Investments in Stock Portfolios and Capital Budgets. *Review of Economics and Statistics* 47 (1), 13–37.

LSEG (2024). *Environmental, social and governance scores from LSEG.* October 2024. LSEG Data & Analytics. www.lseg.com/content/dam/data-analytics/en_us/documents/methodology/lseg-esg-scores-methodology.pdf?ref=zoya-blog (Accessed March 25, 2025).

Luo, X., & Bhattacharya, C.B. (2006). Corporate Social Responsibility, Customer Satisfaction, and Market Value. *Journal of Marketing* 70, 1–18.

Maddala, G.S. (2006). *Introduction to Econometrics*. West Sussex: Wiley.

Malkiel, B.G. (1989). Efficient Market Hypothesis. In J. Eatwell et al. (eds), *Finance. The New Palgrave*. London: Palgrave Macmillan, 127–134.

Malkiel, B.G. (2003). The Efficient Market Hypothesis and Its Critics. *Journal of Economic Perspective* 17 (1), 59–82.

Malkiel, B.G. (2016). *A Random Walk Down Wall Street, the Time-Tested Strategy for Successful Investing*. New York: W.W. Norton.

Mallikarjunappa, T., & Manjunatha, T. (2009). Stock Price Reactions to Dividend Announcements. *Journal of Management & Public Policy* 1 (1), 43–56.

Mandelbrot, B. (1966). Forecasts of Future Prices, Unbiased Markets, and Martingale Models. *Journal of Business* 39 (1), 242–255.

McGowan, M.J. (2010). The Rise of Computerized High Frequency Trading: Use and Controversy. *Duke Law & Technology Review* 016, 1–25.

McKenzie, A.M. (2008). Pre-Harvest Price Expectations for Corn: The Information Content of USDA Reports and New Crop Futures. *American Journal of Agricultural Economics* 90 (2), 351–366.

McWilliams, A., & Siegel, D. (2000). Corporate Social Responsibility and Financial Performance: Correlation or Misspecification? *Strategic Management Journal* 21, 603–609.

Merton, R.C. (1973). An Intertemporal Capital Asset Pricing Model. *Econometrica* 41 (5), 867–888.

Miller, M.H., & Scholes, M. (1972). Rate of Return in Relation to Risk: A Re-Examination of Some Recent Findings. In M.C. Jensen (ed.), *Studies in the Theory of Capital Markets*. New York: Praeger.

Mio, C., Fasan, M., & Scarpa, F. (2023). Materiality Investor Perspectives on Utilities' ESG Performance. An Empirical Analysis of ESG Factors and Cost of Equity. *Utilities Policy* 82, 101555.

Mittal, R.K., Sinha, N., & Singh, A. (2008). An Analysis of Linkage Between Economic Value Added and Corporate Social Responsibility. *Management Decision* 46 (9), 1437–1443.

Moskowitz, M. (1972). Choosing Socially Responsible Stocks. *Business and Society Review* 1, 71–75.

Mossin, J. (1966). Equilibrium in a Capital Asset Market. *Econometrica* 34 (4), 768–783.

Mulialim, C., & Madyan, M. (2023). How Does ESG Explain Excess Returns in Emerging Market? An Asset-Pricing Approach. *Journal of Theoretical and Applied Management* 16 (2), 280–293.

Ngwakwe, C.C. (2008). Environmental Responsibility and Firm Performance: Evidence from Nigeria. *International Journal of Social, Human Science and Engineering* 2 (10), 6–13.

Ogiemudia, O., & Isibor, E. (2021). Testing Weak Form of Efficient Market Hypothesis (EMH) in Nigeria. *Journal of Academic Research in Economics* 13 (3), 488–508.

Oikonomou, I., Brooks, C., & Pavelin, S. (2012). The Impact of Corporate Social Performance on Financial Risk and Utility: A Longitudinal Analysis. *Financial Management* 41 (2), 483–515.

Orlitzky, M., Schmidt, F.L., & Rynes, S.L. (2003). Corporate Social Performance and Financial Performance: A Meta-analysis. *Organization Studies* 24 (3), 403–441.

Patari, S., Arminen, H., Tuppura, A., & Jantunen, A. (2014). Competitive and Responsible? The Relationship Between Corporate Social and Financial Performance in the Energy Sector. *Renewable and Sustainable Energy Reviews* 37, 142–154.

Preston, L.E., & O'Bannon, D.P. (1997). The Corporate Social-Financial Performance Relationship. A Typology and Analysis. *Business and Society* 36 (4), 419–429.

Reilly, F.K., & Drzycimski, E.F. (1981). Short-Run Profits from Stock Splits. *Financial Management 10* (3), 64–74.

Reverte, C. (2012). The Impact of Better Corporate Social Responsibility Disclosure on the Cost of Equity Capital. *Corporate Social Responsibility and Environmental Management* 19, 253–272.

Roberts, H.V. (1959). Stock-Market Patterns and Financial Analysis: Methodological Suggestions. *Journal of Finance 14* (1), 1–10.

Roll, R. (1985). A Note on the Geometry of Shanken CSR T^2 Test for Mean/Variance Efficiency. *Journal of Financial Economics* 14, 349–357.

Rose, A.K., & Selody, J.G. (1984). Exchange Market Efficiency: A Semi-Strong Test Using Multiple Markets and Daily Data. *Review of Economics and Statistics* 66 (4), 669–672.

Rosenberg, B., & Rudd, A. (1982). Factor Related and Specific Returns of Common Stocks: Serial Correlation and Market Efficiency. *Journal of Finance* 37, 543–554.

Roszkowska, P. (2011). *Rewolucja w raportowaniu biznesowym. Interesariusze, konkurencyjność, społeczna odpowiedzialność.* Warsaw (Poland): Difin. Warsaw.

Samuelson, P.A. (1965a). Rational Theory of Warrant Pricing. *Industrial Management Review* 6 (2), 13–39.

Samuelson, P.A. (1965b). Proof that Properly Anticipated Prices Fluctuate Randomly. *Industrial Management Review* 6 (2), 41–49.

Shanken, J. (1985). Multivariate Tests of the Zero-Beta CAPM. *Journal of Financial Economics* 14 (3), 327–348.

Shanken, J. (1992). On the Estimation of Beta-Pricing Models. *Review of Financial Studies* 5 (1), 1–33.

Sharpe, W.F. (1964). Capital Asset Prices: A Theory of Market Equilibrium under Conditions of Risk. *Journal of Finance* 19 (3), 425–442.

Shih, K.-H., Wang, Y.-H., Kao, I.-C., & Lai, F.-M. (2024). Forecasting ETF Performance: A Comparative Study of Deep Learning Models and the Fama-French Three-Factor Model. *Mathematics* 12, 3158.

Shumway, R.H., & Stoffer, D.S. (2011). *Time Series Analysis and Its Applications. With R Examples*. 3rd ed. New York: Springer.

Simerly, R.L. (1995). Institutional, Ownership, Corporate Social Performance, and Firms' Financial Performance. *Psychological Reports* 77, 515–525.

Spelta, A., Pecora, N., Flori, A., & Giudici, P. (2023). The Impact of the SARS-CoV-2 Pandemic on Financial Markets: A Seismologic Approach. *Annals of Operations Research* 330 (1/2), 639–664.

Spicer, B.H. (1978). Investors, Corporate Social Performance and Information Disclosure: An Empirical Study. *The Accounting Review LIII* (1), 94–111.

Stanley, D.J., Kinsman, M.D., Kownatzki, C., & DiLellio, J. (2021). Is the Dow Jones Industrial Average Even Weak-Form Market Efficient? *Journal of Accounting & Finance 21* (1), 159–171.

Sun, L., & Rakhman, F. (2013). CFO Financial Expertise and Corporate Social Responsibility. Evidence from S&P 500 Companies. *International Journal of Law and Management* 55 (3), 161–172.

Tang, Z., Hull, C.E., & Rothenber, S. (2012). How Corporate Social Responsibility Engagement Strategy Moderates the CSR – Financial Performance Relationship. *Journal of Management Studies* 49, 1274–1303.

Treynor, J.L. (1962). Toward a Theory of Market Value of Risky Assets. *Unpublished. Manuscript*, 6. Available at SSRN: https://ssrn.com/abstract=628187

United Nations (1987). *Our Common Future*. Report of the World Commission on Environment and Development. United Nations A/42/427. New York, 4 Aug. 1987. https://digitallibrary.un.org/record/139811?v=pdf

Urbański, S. (2012). Multifactor Explanations of Returns on the Warsaw Stock Exchange in Light of the ICAPM. *Economic Systems 36* (4), 552–570.

Urbański, S., & Zarzecki, D. (2022). The Fama-French Model for Estimating the Cost of Equity Capital: The Impact of Real Options of Investment Projects. *Economic Systems* 46, 1.

Vance, S.C. (1975). Are Socially Responsible Corporations Good Investment Risks? *Management Review* 64 (8), 18–24.

Waddock, S.A., & Graves, S.B. (1997). The Corporate Social Performance – Financial Performance Link. *Strategic Management Journal* 18 (4), 303–319.

Wang, H., Lu, W., Ye, M., Chau, K.W., & Zhang, X. (2016). The Curvilinear Relationship Between Corporate Social Performance and Corporate Financial Performance: Evidence from the International Construction Industry. *Journal of Cleaner Production* 37, 1313–1322.

Yuferova, D. (2024). Algorithmic Trading and Market Efficiency Around the Introduction of the NYSE Hybrid Market. *Journal of Financial Markets* 69, 100909.

Yusoff, H., Mohamad, S.S., & Darus, F. (2013). The Influence of CSR Disclosure Structure on Corporate Financial Performance: Evidence from Stakeholders' Perspective. *Procedia Economics and Finance* 7, 213–220.

Zhou, W. (2022). Is ESG a Novel Pricing Risk Factor for the Chinese Stock Markets during COVID-19? *Proceedings of the 6th International Conference on Economic Management and Green Development (ICEMGD 2022), Part I. 3*. 794–802.

Index

Note: Page numbers in *italics* indicate figures and in **bold** indicate tables on the corresponding pages.

For Product Safety Concerns and Information please contact our EU
representative GPSR@taylorandfrancis.com
Taylor & Francis Verlag GmbH, Kaufingerstraße 24, 80331 München, Germany

www.ingramcontent.com/pod-product-compliance
Ingram Content Group UK Ltd.
Pitfield, Milton Keynes, MK11 3LW, UK
UKHW022039061126
477531UK00009B/429
* 9 7 8 1 0 3 2 9 5 9 6 0 3 *